The English Language in Ireland

Edited by

Diarmaid Ó Muirithe

The Thomas Davis Lecture Series

General Editor: Michael Littleton

Published in collaboration with
Radio Telefís Éireann
by
THE MERCIER PRESS
Cork and Dublin

The Mercier Press Limited
4 Bridge Street, Cork
25 Lower Abbey Street, Dublin 1

The English Language in Ireland
First published 1977
ISBN 0 85342 452 7
© The Mercier Press Limited 1977
Reprinted 1978, 1985

The Thomas Davis Lectures
General Editor: Michael Littleton
Every autumn, winter and spring since September
1953, Radio Telefís Éireann has been broadcasting
half-hour lectures, named in honour of Thomas Davis.
Inspired by one of his famous sayings, 'Educate that
you may be free', the aim of these lectures has been to
provide in popular form what is best in Irish
scholarship and the sciences.

Most of the lectures have been in series; many have
been single broadcasts; some have been in English,
some in Irish. In the time that has passed since they
were initiated, the lectures have dealt with many
aspects and with many centuries of Irish social life,
history, science and literature. The lectures,
distinguished for their special learning at home and
abroad, have been drawn from many nations but
mainly from Ireland.

Printed by Litho Press Co., Midleton, Co. Cork.

CONTENTS

INTRODUCTION

This series of *Thomas Davis Lectures*, broadcast on Radio Telefís Éireann in the winter of 1973, deals with the fortunes of the English language in Ireland since its introduction here. It is not intended to be a comprehensive treatment of 800 years of dialectal development in Ireland; rather is it a collection of papers cn various aspects of that development.

In the introductory lecture, Professor Alan Bliss, of University College, Dublin, traces the historical background to the emergence and growth of what has come to be called Anglo-Irish. Professor P. L. Henry of University College, Galway, deals in the second lecture with the influence of Irish on the kind of English we speak in Ireland today. My own contribution is a lecture on the old dialect of South-East Wexford — a dialect quite unlike modern Anglo-Irish. This dialect became extinct in the mid-nineteenth century.

Mr. Brendan Adams, M.R.I.A., contributes a lecture on the dialects of Ulster, a complex region influenced by Irish and dialectal English and Gaelic imported from Scotland. Seán de Fréine, author of *The Great Silence*, a fine study of the fate of Irish in the nineteenth century, has written about the dominance of English in that century, when a variety of circumstances caused the decline of Irish and the spread of a conservative kind of English throughout the entire country.

Mr. Benedict Kiely, novelist and man of letters, writes on the subject of dialect and literature, and the noted Joycean scholar, Dr. John Garvin, has contributed a lecture on Dublin idiom in the works of major writers. Professor Gordon Quin, of Trinity College, Dublin, the consulting editor of the Royal Irish Academy's recently-completed *Dictionary of the Irish Language,* has written about the collectors of dialect material: Joyce, Poole, Vallency, and the editor of the monumental *English Dialect Dictionary,* Joseph Wright, among others.

Mr. Gerald Delahunty, of the University of California, Irvine, wrote the final lecture in the series. His subject is dialect and local accent, a particularly relevant one, I feel, now that dialects have tended to decline in recent years, due to the fact that the schools and the communications media do not favour the preservation of local speech. Snobbishness has something to do with it, too: there are a great many people who consider dialect and local accent something to be ashamed of, and who don't seem to realise that Standard English has nothing to do with the way people pronounce — that it is a *language,* not an *accent.*

'Language,' Emerson said, 'is fossil poetry': this series of lectures, will, I hope, appeal to all who love words. While we may deplore the misfortunes that almost cost us our own ancestral tongue, it is some slight consolation that we have contributed to the enrichment of our neighbours', and that we have succeeded in moulding and shaping a distinctive Irish speech — Anglo-Irish or Hiberno-English, call it what you will.

Diarmaid Ó Muirithe

Roinn na Nua-Ghaeilge
University College Dublin

THE EMERGENCE OF
MODERN ENGLISH DIALECTS IN IRELAND

ALAN J. BLISS

The English language was first introduced into
Ireland at the time of the Norman invasion in the
twelfth century; the leaders of the invasion no doubt
spoke Norman French, but the majority of their
followers were English-speaking. Neither English nor
French gained much of a foothold except in the towns;
Norman and English settlers were rapidly gaelicised. It
is true that within half a century of the invasion a fairly
substantial body of English poetry had been written in
Ireland, but this was the work of clerics. Within
another half-century a Parliament sitting in Kilkenny
found it necessary to pass the famous *Statutes of
Kilkenny,* which enacted among other things that all
Englishmen must use English surnames, speak English,
and follow English customs, under penalty of forfeiting
their lands. These statutes were ineffective, as such
attempts to impose a language by law always are. The
decline of English was hastened by the Reformation,
since the Irish language became the symbol of the
Catholic religion; during the sixteenth century English
officials visiting Ireland on behalf of the Protestant
régime found that the Catholic settlers refused to speak
English to them. In 1577 Richard Stanihurst observed
that the enemy's language had begun to harbour itself
'like a tetter or ringworm' within the jaws of the

English conquerors.[1] Before 1600 Fynes Moryson noted that

> the English Irish and the very Cittizens (excepting those of Dublin where the lord Deputy resides) though they could speake English as well as wee, yet Commonly speake Irish among themselues, and were hardly induced by our familiar Conversation to speake English with vs, yea Common experience shewed, and my selfe and others often obserued, the Cittizens of Watterford and Corcke hauing wyues that could speake English as well as wee, bitterly to chyde them when they speake English with vs.[2]

By about 1600 the older English survived only in the towns, and in two widely-separated rural areas. One of these areas consisted of the two Wexford baronies of Forth and Bargy, where a distinctive dialect survived until well into the nineteenth century; Diarmaid Ó Muirithe will be telling us more about this elsewhere in this book. The other was the district north of Dublin known as Fingal, 'a little Territory,' as Fynes Moryson tells us, 'as it were the Garner of the Kingdome, which is enuironed by the Sea and great Riuers, and this situation hath defended it from the incursions of Rebels in former ciuill warres.'[3] Here a distinctive dialect survived until about 1800. In 1691 Sir William Petty observed that the dialect of Fingal was similar to that of Wexford but not identical to it.[4] In the 1770s Arthur Young heard the dialect spoken near Balbriggan, and explained that the Fingalians were 'an english colony planted here many years ago, speaking nearly the same language as the barony of Forth, but more intermixed with irish in language, &c., from vicinity to the capital.'[5] This last rather surprising comment makes it clear that in the eighteenth century Irish must have been extensively spoken in Dublin.

In the towns the older English certainly survived throughout most of the seventeenth century;

unfortunately we have very little information about what it was like. The only evidence available is to be found in the speech of Irish characters in Elizabethan and Jacobean plays, and much of this evidence is visibly quite untrustworthy. Most of the plays were written by Englishmen who knew nothing of Ireland, and it seems clear that already at this early date a conventional 'stage Irish' had been established. One play, however, is an exception: this is the (play of *Captain Thomas Stukeley,*) entered in the Stationers' Registers in 1600, and printed in 1605; there is some evidence that it was first performed in 1596.[6] Thomas Stukeley was not a fictional character, but an English adventurer who engaged in military exploits in various parts of the world. According to the play he took part in the defence of Dundalk when it was besieged by Shane O'Neill in May 1566. By some curious chance the scene which deals with the siege of Dundalk has survived in two different versions, printed one after the other in the edition of 1605. The two versions have effectively the same content, but the first is in blank verse and in English, and the second is in prose and in broad Anglo-Irish dialect. The reason for the survival of the two versions, and the problem of priority between them, have been much discussed; it is by no means certain that the author of the dialect scene was the same as the author of the rest of the play. Fortunately we need not concern ourselves with all this; all that matters for our purpose is the probability that the dialect version really represents the English spoken in the Irish towns about 1600. The writer, whoever he was, seems to display accurate knowledge of the neighbourhood of Dundalk. Significantly, the scene is fairly liberally sprinkled with Irish words and phrases correctly used. The presence of Irish words and phrases is not in itself any proof of special knowledge, since they occur also in the plays of English dramatists, and seem to have formed part of

conventional 'stage Irish'; but English writers often get
them wrong. Thus Thomas Dekker, in his play *The
Honest Whore,* uses the phrase *slán leat* where an
Irishman would say *slán agat*; in *Stukeley* both
phrases are used, and they are correctly distinguished.
Most important of all, the writer of the dialect scene
uses an Irish word which (if it has been correctly
identified) belongs specifically to Oriel Irish;[7] that is, it
might have been heard in Dundalk, but hardly in any
other town. It seems reasonable to assume that the
writer really knew Dundalk, and that his representation
of urban Anglo-Irish dialect can be accepted as
accurate.

If we examine the kind of English represented in this
scene, we find first of all that it bears a considerable
resemblance to the English of the Wexford baronies as
it was recorded two hundred years later, and this
strengthens our confidence in the accuracy of the
representation. The characteristic features are
conservatism of pronunciation and strong Irish
influence. Both features can be observed in the word
féete, meaning 'white'. The pronunciation of the vowel
represents extreme conservatism: in England the
original sound /i:/ had been replaced by /əi/ soon after
1400. The substitution of *f* for *wh* illustrates Irish
influence: the unfamiliar English sound was replaced
by the Irish 'broad' *f* which is similar to it. As we shall
see, conservatism and Irish influence are both
characteristic of present-day Anglo-Irish; nevertheless,
the dialect represented in *Stukeley* cannot possibly be
the ancestor of the present-day dialect. For one thing,
the conservatism in *Stukeley* goes back to an
altogether earlier stage in the history of the English
language; for another, the Irish influence is of a
different kind. As far as pronunciation is concerned,
Irish influence tends to result in the substitution of Irish
sounds for unfamiliar English sounds; but the
substitution may work in different ways, as we can see

from the examination of English words borrowed into the Irish language at various periods. As might be expected, present-day Anglo-Irish follows the same pattern as the more recent loanwords in Irish; the older dialect seems to follow the pattern of the older loanwords. Thus, it would be surprising now to hear such pronunciations as *shecretary* for 'secretary', or *blesh* for 'bless', both indicated in *Stukeley;* but this treatment of the English *s*-sound is exactly what we find in the older loanwords in Irish, like *seirbhís* for 'service'.

We do not know exactly how long this older type of English survived in the towns, nor by what process it was replaced by a more modern type of Anglo-Irish. Something very similar was used as late as 1663 in an indecent play called *Hic et Ubique; or, the Humors of Dublin*; but this was written by Richard Head, who spent most of his life in London, and the dialect he uses may have been conventional; for all we know, he may have used *Stukeley* as a basis for his usage. It is by no means impossible that something of the older urban English survives in the modern urban dialects; certainly the dialects of Dublin, Belfast and Cork have features in common which they do not share with any rural dialects; this is a question which deserves further investigation.

There is no direct external evidence bearing on the origin and emergence of the present-day Anglo-Irish dialects, and we have to fall back on internal, linguistic evidence. The dialects of Ulster present special problems, and Brendan Adams will be telling us about them later; if we leave them out of account, we can say that in general the dialects of the other three provinces go back to the English of about 1650; their ancestor was a sub-Standard, probably dialectal, form of English. The evidence for this statement is to be found primarily in the realm of pronunciation. There is no point in our comparing the actual sounds used in Anglo-Irish with the sounds used in English at various periods; as we have seen, there is a tendency for Irish sounds to be substituted for English sounds, and these have in general survived. We can, however, compare the distribution of the sounds. We can, for instance, note that *wh* is still distinguished from *w* in Anglo-Irish, and that *r* is still pronounced where it is lost in standard English. The details of the analysis are complex, but the result is clear; and it is confirmed by the evidence of vocabulary. Many seventeenth-century words are still preserved in Anglo-Irish, such as *cog* 'to cheat in an examination', or *delph* 'crockery'. Dialectal origin is also confirmed by the number of dialectal words still used in Ireland.

The date to which linguistic evidence leads us fits in well enough with historical considerations. It is easy to see how the Cromwellian settlement of the 1650s, by which native landowners were removed to Connacht, while Leinster and Munster were occupied by English planters, would have ensured the wide diffusion of the English of that period. It is easy to see, too, why this type of English should not have been much influenced by subsequent developments in England. Before the Act of Union of 1800 there was relatively little travel between England and Ireland; we have to imagine the planters as remaining on their own estates, rarely meeting anyone but their planter neighbours and their Irish servants and tenants. As time went on their speech seemed more and more conservative, and it was increasingly subject to the influence of Irish speech-habits. The growing conservatism was not, of course, an active process; it was merely that continuing developments in the speech of England left a wider and wider gap between the two types of language. The influence of Irish, on the other hand, was not only active but cumulative. At first the influence of Irish was mainly selective and preservative: where there was a choice of English words and idioms, one would be

preferred to another because it had some support in
Irish usage. Later the influence became more direct:
Irish idioms were introduced which had no analogy at
all in English usage. Professor Henry will be telling us
more about this.

The extent of Irish influence on the language of the
planters may seem surprising, but the fact is not in
doubt. On this point we have the very valuable
evidence of Swift, who castigates the kind of English
spoken two generations after the Cromwellian
plantations in his burlesque pieces, *A Dialogue in
Hybernian Stile* and *Irish Eloquence*.[8] These are not
independent compositions; they consist of substantially
the same material differently arranged, in the first in
dialogue form, in the second in the form of a letter;
they can conveniently be treated as one. In the
Dialogue the two speakers are plainly landowners, as a
comic interchange reveals:

> 'You have a Country-house, are you [a]
> Planter[?]'
> 'Yes, I have planted a great many Oak trees,
> and Ash trees, and some Elm-trees round a
> Lough.'

Yet, though the speakers are landowners, their
language is very strongly influenced by Irish. In some
fifty lines there are no less than seventeen Irish words.
More important still, there are at least three sentences
more or less literally translated from Irish idiom: *Pray,
how does he get his health?*, meaning 'What kind of
health does he enjoy?'; *It is kind Father for you*,
meaning 'You have inherited that tendency from your
father'; *I wonder what is gone with them*, meaning 'I
wonder what has happened to them.' The importance
of these three sentences can hardly be over-estimated.
The Irish words, numerous though they are, could
have been picked up casually, just as an English tourist

might readily pick up such a word as *loch*; but the sentences quoted reflect the usage of someone who is thinking in Irish but speaking in English. Since the planters themselves would not think in Irish, they can only have picked up such idioms through daily intercourse with English-speaking Irishmen. No doubt most of the planters must as babies have been cared for by Irish nurses, and in their childhood they would have fraternised with the children of their servants, but the Irish influence on their language seems too extensive to be accounted for in this way; we must rather envisage such a situation as [Maria Edgeworth describes in *Castle Rackrent,* where the supposed narrator of the story, the steward Thady Quirk, is throughout the confidant and adviser of his masters.]

Some of the hibernicisms ridiculed by Swift can still be heard in common speech: despite the archaisms, there is a very modern ring about such a sentence as 'Pray lend me a lone of your last news paper till I read it over.' Other usages are hibernicisms no longer, since they have passed over into the common stock of English. It is difficult at first glance to see anything out of the ordinary in such a sentence as 'His Lady has been very Unwell.' However, the word *unwell* was not in common use in England until about 1785. It was first introduced into England by Lord Chesterfield, who wrote: 'I am what you call in Ireland, and a very good expression I think it is, *unwell.*'[9]

In his burlesques Swift makes no attempt to indicate any distinctive kind of pronunciation, but elsewhere he refers to the deleterious effects, not only of learning Irish, but even of pronouncing Irish place-names:

> How is it possible that a gentleman who lives in those parts where the *town-lands* (as they call them) of his estate produce such odious sounds from the mouth, the throat, and the nose, can be able to repeat the words without dislocating

every muscle that is used in speaking, and
without applying the same tone to all other
words, in every language he understands; as it is
plainly to be observed not only in those people of
the better sort who live in Galway and the
Western parts, but in most counties of Ireland?
. . . What we call the *Irish brogue* is no sooner
discovered, than it makes the deliverer in the last
degree ridiculous and despised; and, from such a
mouth, an Englishman expects nothing but bulls,
blunders, and follies.[10]

The word *brogue* was, in fact, first used as early as
1689, only a generation after the Cromwellian
settlement. We can find some details of what was
meant by the brogue in Thomas Sheridan's *Dictionary
of the English Language,* published in Dublin in 1780;
Sheridan devotes two closely-printed pages of his
Introduction to a discussion of the 'mistakes' of
pronunciation made by the 'well-educated natives of
Ireland'.[11] He notes three main tendencies, only one of
which can still be observed in Ireland, and that not in
the mouths of educated speakers. Irishmen, Sheridan
tells us, pronounce words like *tea, sea, please,* as *tay,
say, plays;* this pronunciation is still common enough
in rural areas, but it is avoided by educated speakers.
Secondly, he tells us that the Irish pronounce *patron,
matron* as *pahtron, mahtron;* this pronunciation is no
longer heard, but it is perhaps comparable with the
present-day pronunciation of *status, data* as *stahtus,
dahta.* The third type of pronunciation noted by
Sheridan seems to have left no trace at all: he tells us
that the 'well-educated native' pronounces words like
calm, psalm as *cawm, psawm.* In addition to these
three general tendencies, Sheridan lists 55 individual
words whose pronunciation in Ireland differs from
English usage; most of the pronunciations he indicates
are still in common use.

So far we have been considering the characteristics of the English used by the landlord class; now we must examine the further development which this language underwent in the mouths of native Irishmen. It is remarkably difficult to determine the number of English-speakers in Ireland at any date before the first language census in 1851; and by that time the picture had been distorted by the widespread death and emigration resulting from the Famine. Richard Edgeworth, Maria Edgeworth's father, wrote in 1811 that the Irish peasantry 'have within these few years made a greater progress in learning English, than the Welsh have made since the time of Edward the First, in acquiring the language'. Rough figures compiled by Christopher Anderson in 1828 suggest that in the eastern half of the country more than 50% of the people were indeed English-speaking; but in the western half less than 50%, and in most of Connacht less than 10% were English-speaking.[12] We shall not go far wrong if we assume that the general acquisition of the English language by the people of Ireland hardly began until after 1800. Yet we have seen that already in the time of Swift the language of the landlords had been strongly influenced by the usage of English-speaking Irishmen. No doubt the servants of the landlords, their stewards, grooms, and gardeners, must at an early date have acquired some fluency in English, while the vast mass of tenants still spoke no language but Irish.

One fact is of vital importance for the history of Anglo-Irish dialects: the Irishman learning English had no opportunity of learning it from speakers of standard English. Within quite a short time after the Cromwellian settlement the language of the planters had become so distinctive that those who spoke it became 'ridiculous and despised'. After the Act of Union there was much more traffic between Dublin and London, and the rise of the English public schools in the 1830s meant that the landlords increasingly tended to send their children to school in England; the present so-called 'Ascendancy accent' reflects the English public-school accent, usually accompanied by a penetrating quality of voice rarely heard in England. However, by the time the landlord class had learned to speak something approximating to standard English, the social cleavage had become absolute, so that intercourse between landlord and tenant was minimal. The title-page of *Castle Rackrent* states that the novel describes 'the manners of the Irish squires, before the year 1782', and in her Preface Maria Edgeworth assures us again that 'the manners depicted in the following pages are not those of the present age'; in the nineteenth century the free and easy relationship between the steward Thady Quirk and his masters would scarcely have been possible.

Irishmen learning English, therefore, had to rely on teachers of their own race, whose own English was very different from standard English, so that there was nothing to check the progressive influence of the Irish language. In each generation the speech of the teachers was already strongly influenced by Irish, the speech of the learners even more so. The teaching of English was at first in the hands of the hedge schoolmasters, and later (after 1831) of the national schoolmasters, the first of whom were themselves the product of the hedge schools. It would be interesting to know more in detail about the organisation of the hedge schools, but it seems certain that the system was self-perpetuating. The intelligent boy who wished to become a schoolmaster himself would continue at his own local school until his own master could teach him no more; then he would set out as a 'poor scholar' and travel from school to school, learning something more at each. In due course he would look for some district where there was a demand for education, and set up a school of his own. At no stage would he have the opportunity of learning English from a speaker of standard English. Furthermore, he would be partly self-taught. To improve his knowledge of English he would read widely; in the course of his reading he would meet many technical and learned words which he would never have heard pronounced; he had to invent a pronunciation for them, a pronunciation commonly based on the spelling, which in English is a notoriously untrustworthy guide. Sometimes he might be uncertain of the meaning, and would have to puzzle it out for himself from the context; usually he would be right, but occasionally he might be wrong.

These considerations explain two noteworthy features of the Anglo-Irish dialect. One is the tendency for Irishmen to stress a different syllable from the one stressed in standard English. So, for instance, the Irishman says *discípline, laméntable, architécture*, where the Englishman says *díscipline, lámentable, árchitecture*. In some cases the Irish stress seems to represent the survival of an older English stress, but in many cases there is no historical justification for it, and we must fall back on the invented pronunciations of the hedge schoolmaster. The other feature is a tendency towards malapropism — the use of the wrong word, or the use of a word in a meaning it does not have in standard English. This tendency can be observed in any part of Ireland, but it is especially common in Dublin, and O'Casey makes extensive use of it in his plays: *formularies* for 'formalities', for instance, or *declivity* for 'proclivity'. Some of these are, no doubt, just slips, but some of them recur, and may be due to an erroneous interpretation by some hedge schoolmaster.

Finally, perhaps the most remarkable feature of the present-day Anglo-Irish dialects is their relative uniformity. Of course there are regional differences; it is usually possible to recognise from a man's accent what part of the country he comes from. Yet in the three southern provinces, at least, there are fewer basic differences than one might expect. In areas where Irish has long been lost, Irish influence is still strong, because English has been handed down from teacher to pupil in unbroken tradition since the days when Irish was still spoken; and in areas where Irish has only recently given place to English, the English used is very conservative, because the language of the teachers was itself conservative. Provided he does not try to ape the speech of others, the Irishman has at his command a form of language which distinguishes him from all other speakers of English, and which accurately reflects the social history of his country.

NOTES

1. Richard Stanihurst, 'The description of Irelande', in Raphaell Holinshed, *The Firste volume of the Chronicles of England, Scotlande, and Irelande* (1577) f.3 col.3.

2. Charles Hughes, *Shakespeare's Europe: Unpublished Chapters of Fynes Moryson's Itinerary* (1903) 213.

3. *An Itinerary written by Fynes Moryson, Gent.* (1617) 158.

4. Sir William Petty, *The Political Anatomy of Ireland* (1691) 106.

5. Arthur Young, *A Tour in Ireland* (1780) 95.

6. Philip Henslowe refers to a new play *Stewtley*, acted by the Admiral's Men on 11 December 1596; see *Henslowe's Diary*, edited by W. W. Greg.

7. The word is spelt *booygh*, apparently Irish *buidheach*, an Oriel variant of *bideach* 'small'.

8. Herbert Davis, *The Prose Works of Jonathan Swift* iv (1957) 277-9.

9. Lord Chesterfield, Letters to his Son (1774) 8 October 1755.

10. 'On Barbarous Denominations in Ireland', *Prose Works* iv (1957) 280-4.

11. Thomas Sheridan, *A General Dictionary of the English Language* (1780) p. lxvi.

12. Christopher Anderson, *Historical Sketches of the Ancient Native Irish* (1828) 143-64.

ANGLO-IRISH AND ITS IRISH BACKGROUND

P. L. HENRY

Three major strands are woven together in the English of Ireland: Firstly, a characteristically rural variety compounded of Irish and English or Irish and Scots. This developed chiefly in the last century and a half and is properly called Anglo-Irish. Secondly, a more urban, regional and standard variety tending towards international or so-called Standard English. This derives ultimately from British settlers in Ireland and its germinal period was the seventeenth century. It is properly called Hiberno-English. The third strand is Ulster Scots from the same period.

The term Anglo-Irish appears to have been first applied to the English *people* of Ireland and thence to their literature and language. As an inclusive term for that language and literature it fails to win universal approval. Some would replace it by *Hiberno-English* for the language and others by Irish for the literature, which on the whole tends to muddle what is otherwise a reasonably-clear picture. In order to judge the fitness of names it is first necessary to examine the things they stand for. It is precisely my purpose here to convey as clearly as possible what Anglo-Irish essentially is. Such problems as the proper use of the name should then cease to give trouble.

The outcome of war in Ireland in the seventeenth century was the split society of the eighteenth in which the winner proceeded to take all. The winner was the English Protestant colonist, the loser the Irish Catholic native. It became a rule of privilege versus deprivation and disability. English became the language of politics, of public service, of commerce and of education. Irish clung to the countryside remote from where the action was. If you give a people who are not particularly dull one century to learn the lesson, you may expect that they will put it into practice when the day comes. It was not yet clear that the day would come, but the nineteenth century made it crystal clear that acquiring the language of privilege could be a key to survival in a land apparently forsaken by Providence.

In other words, the loss of political freedom in the seventeenth century was followed by deprivation of civil rights in the eighteenth. This led, inevitably in the circumstances, to deprivation on the cultural and spiritual level in the nineteenth.

The policy of replacing the Irish language by English, a policy frequently reiterated by Dublin statesmen from the fourteenth century on, got under way with the national schools under their clerical managers from 1831. Prior to the founding of Maynooth in 1795 Irish clergy had been trained on the continent in a surreptitious manner. There was nothing there to weaken their grip on their own particular way of life and world view which a language characteristically represents and preserves. On the contrary the encounter with continental languages would serve to inculcate a conscious sense of what their own Irish language stood for. The founding of Maynooth to train Catholic clergy weakened a link which had lasted one thousand years. It left the Irish-speaking community isolated on the edge of the English-speaking block and depending on it for their education. What they learned from it was, naturally, that they and all they represented were inferior, unfashionable, and gross; moreover they were impoverished. Were they to improve, they must copy their urban brethren who spoke English. In time they would acquire their prejudices, embedded in the language.

Even so the replacement of Irish by English could not have proceeded among a people once proud of their language and conscious of their traditions and culture without favouring circumstances. The reduced economic condition of the people and the dreadful disasters of the nineteenth century in Ireland ravaged the race physically and spiritually. I use the word *race* here to bring home the fact that for the first time in history the native Irish stock were faced with the prospect of their physical extinction as a separate people. Having referred to the physical basis of race I hasten to add that this is not its definitive element, but that race properly denotes cultural and spiritual affinities and can incorporate people of diverse national origins. Since the word was misapplied in Nazi Germany in the thirties, people have tended to steer clear of it or have adopted it as a mere term of abuse in its wrong meaning.

From the middle of the nineteenth century flight became the keyword, flight from the land, from the country, from the language. A parish priest would provide his flock with a gratuitous symbol for the Irish mother heard speaking the native language to her children. It would not be complimentary. In the school a child reported for speaking Irish would have the tally-stick (called *bata scóir*) hanging from his neck notched up to date, or might stand in a corner with a wooden gag (called *priaslach*) between his teeth. A pronounced inferiority complex about speaking Irish set in which symbolised the doubt — will we survive as a race? In the twentieth century the same complex persists in association with the question, will we survive as a nation? So let's be on the winning side and as ambivalent as possible.

The Gaeltacht today still provides a vantage ground from which linguistic developments in rural Ireland in the last 200 years can be surveyed. That is to say, though things have changed, the essence of a bilingual situation remains in many places. What are the outstanding characteristics of the bilingual situation in Ireland? First of all, it is found in a fuller sense only in the Gaeltacht and its surroundings. A fuller sense means inheriting two languages rather than learning one of them. The next point is that the sexes react differently to a bilingual situation. This I have observed not only in Ireland but along the Atlantic seaboard from North Spain to Iceland. The men are more conservative and prefer the native language though it be the less fashionable, which usually means the weaker. Girls tend to adopt the fashionable foraging language, Spanish among the Basques, American among the Icelanders. Women in the Kerry Gaeltacht tend to move over and back or in and out of the two languages alternately: they mingle them, rather than separate them, in animated conversation. This does not mean that they cannot keep them apart if they so wish, but that, in fact, they do not normally do so. A condition is, of course, a good knowledge of English, which is naturally commoner among the younger people. A man surveying the damp wintry landscape before breakfast from his bedroom window may give vent to his depression *What's it all for, nó cad chuige é ar ao' chor?* the same remark is made in both languages bridged by the transition word *nó* meaning 'or'. It has an interesting rhetorical impact. So what, you may say! In fact, this is the mode of the macaronic songs and ballads like the famous *Carrickfergus* which develop their narrative theme with equal-handed justice in the two languages. The bilingual ballad is an obvious product of the nineteenth century and as we have seen, it is based on the living reality.

There are adequate examples on record of typical nineteenth-century efforts to speak the foreign tongue. On the whole these are of the homemade rough-hewn variety, tentative fragments loosely put together which convey their meaning in a hit-and-miss manner. For example a County Clare boy grumbles about how little milk he was given at table and his father replies impatiently *Drink what's that in your noggin, you bacach, and you'll get more while ago when you'll drink what's that.* This parent would speak Irish to his wife but not to his children, on the grounds that they would need English for survival. His effort looks like an improvisation based on what he has heard in the nearest market town. He doesn't understand the phrase *a while ago* and the phrase *what's that* shows uncertainty about English demonstratives. This speaker would use much of his Irish vocabulary in his improvisations, linking his phrases after the Irish fashion. Judging by older Gaeltacht speakers of today his English enunciation would be clipped, with a tendency to separate the words as if his speech organs found difficulty coping with them.

One of the reasons why sentences such as the above are recorded and rehearsed is that they were found amusing later by people who had made progress in learning English. However, from a linguistic point of view they are vastly more interesting than the ordinary conventional kind which is learned or acquired by imitation; because they show the creative spirit at work forging an instrument for personal use, rather than adopting it ready-made from others. What I am suggesting in fact is that creating Anglo-Irish is a different thing from learning English. Or to put the matter differently, what the Irish people set out to do was to learn English; what they managed by 1900 was to create Anglo-Irish, which Hyde, Yeats, Synge, Lady Gregory and the others found to be a vastly more stimulating and worthwhile achievement. It may be added that these writers, working by intuition, were the only group in the country to grasp that the mind of the people working for decades on new material had forged a new language which could develop a literature in its own right. This understanding is what underlies the literary work of Synge.   A normal development would have been to adopt the new language at the appropriate level for all other spheres of activity inside Ireland. This is what occurred in thirteenth and fourteenth-century England when the native language had been displaced by French: the newcomers were absorbed and the people hammered out and adopted the new French-English. But circumstances favoured this and favoured the growth of an independent English spirit. Whereas in nineteenth-century Ireland the colonist stock held the reins, the tie with England was close and there was no scope for the rise of Anglo-Irish as a national speech norm fashioned by the people and therefore adapted to their own needs, educational, social and political. The situation is symbolised by an Education Machine which could not understand the *creation* but only the *imitation* and learning of language.

We are now ready to consider a representative specimen of Anglo-Irish text as a basis for our analysis and description of that language. The text is from current speech in an area of County Galway. It is close to what Synge must have encountered there at the beginning of the century, a pocket of the old traditional Anglo-Irish holding out in the company of spoken Irish. The fact that the speakers are bilingual enables us to place an Irish version of every sentence beside the Anglo-Irish. The version called Standard English represents an effort to arrive at an English version close in form and meaning to the Anglo-Irish. It seems no less marvellous to come across Anglo-Irish of this kind today than it is to encounter in so many places still an Irish spoken in the traditional manner with great richness and force.

The text is in the form of a dialogue between locals on the themes of marriage and death. It may, of course, be found interesting from the human and social point of view; but our object is to stimulate the listener to observe what kinds of contribution each of the two languages Irish and English have been called upon to make to the forging of each Anglo-Irish sentence. Indeed some of the sentences will test the reader's knowledge of Anglo-Irish until the Irish or English version solves his difficulty for him. It may be objected to some of the English versions that they are more formal and less colloquial than the Anglo-Irish text, and this should be taken into account when comparing the three. N.B. *Standard English* does not mean *Southern British!*

First Context: The Theme is Marriage

Did you know that for years before they married they used to meet at the wooden gate?

Anglo-Irish comment: *'Tis an aise to the gate they to be married.*

Irish equivalent: *Is mór an suaimhneas don gheata iad a bheith pósta.*

Standard English version: *It's a relief to the gate that they're married.*

Most ordinary Irish people will readily understand the Anglo-Irish sentence *'Tis an aise to the gate they to be married.* As soon as I turn to Standard English I am faced with the crux that such a conception as this rarely if ever seeks accommodation in English outside an Irish context. Granted, you might expect *What a relief to the gate!* in a comparable situation, but whatever this might convey — or be intended to convey — it is a balder statement, lacking the articulated reference of the Anglo-Irish and also of course its stylistic quality.

If you observe to a speaker of Standard English outside Ireland, whether he be English, American, Australian or otherwise *It's a relief to the gate that they're married* in the above context he will undoubtedly raise at least one puzzled eyebrow at such an unEnglish approach to experience or at such an unusual quality of humour at work upon his language. You will be obliged to concede on reflection that languages are distinctive in the first instance because they embody contrasting views of life; and secondly because they employ their own favoured linguistic modes to mediate their particular world view. It follows that a one-to-one relationship between, say, German and French, or English and Irish, cannot exist, and that a word-for-word translation from one to the other such as we see so often in public is a meaningless exercise.

The sentence *'Tis an aise to the gate they to be married* has a delicacy which commends it from a human point of view and a balanced structure which appeals from the literary. It does not lack elegance. All this becomes clear in the light of such vulgar and unmanageable phrases at second hand from literate Dublin as the one about trees 'more sinned against than sinning'. We shall not conclude on such slim evidence that the product of the unlettered milieu is nearer to literature. In fact however, this is what the Anglo-Irish writers already mentioned discovered when they went to the people at the beginning of the century to renew themselves for their literary task.

Before Dublin town had put on the alarming aspect of a European metropolis it was known as a place where the myth flourished, especially in academic circles. One recognises the genre still, when one hears of the distinguished visitor to RTÉ, imbued with a missionary zeal, confronting a wall map of Ireland with his cigarette holder launched in a wide encircling move: *Our task* (he says) *is to spread sophistication from here* (the Irish Sea) *to here* (the Atlantic). The myth makers would ask: Who did you say was unsophisticated? and, What is it you would really like to spread?

To return to context number one: The two are married. A friend of the bride's observes that she herself was present at the celebration in the bride's new home shortly after the wedding. This event is called *the risin'-out,* in Irish *an t-éirí amach;* in County Roscommon it is known as the *dhraggin' home.* Now this was her comment:

Anglo-Irish: *I was below at her risin'-out.*
Irish equivalent: *Bhí mé thíos ag a héirí amach.*
Standard English version: Problematical!

A smooth rendering does not seem possible, for there seems to be no standard English equivalent for the celebration in question, or for the use of *below* in the sense 'north of here'. Anglo-Irish *below*/Irish *thíos* both refer to a direction northwards of the speaker, in keeping with the Irish system of indicating position relative to the speaker by means of cardinal points or their representatives; for instance westwards is 'back', eastwards 'over', southwards 'up (above)' and northwards 'down (below)' as in our example.

So she says: *I was below at her risin'-out,* and she adds:

Anglo-Irish: *'Twas Nora that shtood to her.*
Irish equivalent: *'Sí Nóra a sheas léithe.*
Standard English version: *Nora was her bridesmaid.*

Second Context

In Shrovetide a man seeking a wife would go matchmaking to the house of the girl he wished to marry, bringing one or two others along; or he might send the others in his stead. It was usual to bring a bottle of whiskey to oil and seal the bargain. The local Irish term for a matchmaking foray of the kind is the non-committal *ar bóthar,* literally and Anglo-Irish *on road*; just as one says in Anglo-Irish *He's on the road continually* for 'he's on the move'. The marriage market is, of course, a burning topic, so we have the question:

Anglo-Irish: *Did-ya-hear of anna wan bein' on road?*
Irish equivalent: *Ar airigh tú éinne bheith ar bóthar?*

Standard English version: *Have you heard of anyone going matchmaking?*

A suitor is mentioned, and his quarry:

Anglo-Irish: *He axed her a'right but they wouldn't put her in it.*

Irish equivalent: *D'iarr sé í ach ní chuirfeadh siad ann í.*

Standard English version: *He asked for her hand in marriage but her family refused as his farm was below the standard they expected.*

Note how much background clarification is required for the non-Irish audience.

The conversation continues:

Anglo-Irish: *She has no tóir on a match.*

Irish equivalent: *Níl aon tóir aici ar chleamhnas.*

Standard English version: *She is not seeking a husband.*

A more distinguished suitor is in question for her, and the conversation proceeds:

Anglo-Irish: *Faith, she's gettin' a good place.*

Irish equivalent: *M'anam go bhfuil sí a' fáil áit mhaith.*

Standard English version: *She's marrying into a good farm.*

Anglo-Irish: *If she is itsel', she's good enough to 'im.*

Irish equivalent: *Má tá fhéin, tá sí sách maith aige.*

Standard English version: *Even so, she is his equal socially.*

The man, however, is thought to be rather advanced in age, as appears from:

Anglo-Irish: *He's pinshin age if 'e's thrushtin' to it.*

Irish equivalent: *Tá sé aois a' phinsin má tá sé a' taobhú leis.*

Standard English version: *He's of pensionable age, (70), if not more.*

This is disputed:

Anglo-Irish: *He has fair age but he's not the 70 all out.*

Irish equivalent: *Tá aois mhaith aige ach níl sé baileach na trí scóir is deich.*

Standard English version: *He's rather old but not quite
    70.*

He is held to be a good match in spite of his age:

Anglo-Irish: *Whatever age has 'e, she never'll get
    betther if she don't take 'im.*

Irish equivalent: *Is cuma cén aois é, ní bhfaigh' sí níos
    fearr ná é, mara bpósfaidh sí é.*

Standard English version: *Whatever his age, she won't
    better herself elsewhere.*

But why should she fuss about his age?

Anglo-Irish: *Isn't it all aequal to 'er what age has 'e, so
    long as she's gettin' a good place.*

Irish equivalent: *Nach cuma dhuithe cén aois atá aige
    nuair atá sí a' fáil áit mhaith.*

Standard English version: *It is surely beside the point
    how old he may be provided his farm is right.*

The size of his bank account is adverted to:

Anglo-Irish: *They say 'tidn't known what money he has
    in bank.*

Irish equivalent: *Deir siad nach bhfuil 'fhios céard 'tá
    sa mbanc aige.*

Standard English version: *He is reputed to have a vast
    sum in the bank.*

In fact the man inherited it:

Anglo-Irish: *It was a good place ever; there was oul'
    money in that house.*

Irish equivalent: *Bhí an áit sin go maith riamh; bhí
    sean-airgead sa teach sin.*

Standard English version: *It was always a prosperous
    farm; the family were well-off for generations.*

Anglo-Irish: *There no word o' a lie in it.*

Irish equivalent: *Níl aon fhocal bréige ann.*

Standard English version: *That (this) is quite true*
    [which, of course, is a different approach].

Unfortunately, however, the match is being opposed:

Anglo-Irish: *They say her brothers are puttin' agin it.*

Irish equivalent: *Deir siad go bhfuil a driotháireachaí
    a' cur ina aghaidh.*

Standard English version: *Her brothers are said to be opposing it.*

Anglo-Irish: *The mosht fau't they have on 'im is counta him bein' so ould.*

Irish equivalent: *'Sé 'n locht is mó atá acu air, mar gheall air é bheith chomh sean sin.*

Standard English version: *Their chief objection to him is his age.*

The latest news is that the match is off: *broke up* is the term used. Rumour is already busied with it:

Anglo-Irish: *The mosht way it was broke up, he was axin' too much money wit' 'er.*

Irish equivalent: *'Sé 'n fáth is mó gur briseadh suas é, bhí sé ag iarra' an iomarca airgid léithi.*

Standard English version: *The main reason for the failure to proceed was that he was asking too large a dowry.*

Anglo-Irish: *He's verra near 'imsel'.*

Irish equivalent: *Tá sé an-ghar dhó fhéin.*

Standard English version: *He's very mean.*

Anglo-Irish: *There's misfortune shook down on 'im.*

Irish equivalent: *Tá 'n mí-ádh craití anuas air.*

Standard English version: *He's very unlucky.*

Anglo-Irish: *They'll a'ways be misfortune on the same fella.*

Irish equivalent: *Beidh mí-ádh i gcónaí ar a' bhfear céanna.*

Standard English version: *That man will always be unfortunate.*

And now to another theme. The fact that matches were often discussed at wakes reflects the link felt to exist between the two vital events, marriage and death. Our second theme is death. The poor man in question was in failing health, or simply *failing,* for a period, and the course of his illness was noted in some detail:

Anglo-Irish: *He was fallin' back wit' a while.*

Irish equivalent: *Bhí sé a' titim siar le scatha'.*

Standard English version: *His health was declining for some time.*

Anglo-Irish: *He idn't too good those days.*

Irish equivalent: *Níl sé an-mhaith na laetheantaí seo.*

Standard English version: *He's not very well just now/He hasn't been well for the past few days.*

Anglo-Irish: *He wants as good as he is* or *he wants how good'e is* or *he wants how 'e is.*

Irish equivalent: *Ní mór 'ó mar 'tá sé.*

Standard English version: *He is none too well.*

Anglo-Irish: *He's not gettin' his health at all right.*

Irish equivalent: *Níl sé a' fáilt a shláinte ceart 'chor ar bith.*

Standard English version: *He is not in good health.*

Anglo-Irish: *He's complainin' a long time.*

Irish equivalent: *Tá sé ag éagaoineadh le fada.*

Standard English version: *He's ailing a long time.*

Anglo-Irish: *He's lookin' half-shlack enough.*

Irish equivalent: *Tá sé a' breathnú leathleicí go leor.*

Standard English version: *He is not looking too well.*

Anglo-Irish: *There's no death on 'im, I'd say.*

Irish equivalent: *Níl aon bhás air, déarfainn.*

Standard English version: *I expect he'll recover all right.*

Anglo-Irish: *He's given over for death; they have no hopes out o' im.*

Irish equivalent: *Tá sé tabharthaí suas dhon bhás; níl aon tsúil acu leis.*

Standard English version: *They do not expect him to recover.*

In the event the patient did die, and the conversation at his funeral took the following turn:

Anglo-Irish: *They had no thinkin' at all o' the death.*

Irish equivalent: *Ní ra' aon smaointiú 'bith acu ar a' mbás.*

Standard English version: *His death took them unawares.*

Anglo-Irish: *He earned the death verra hard.*

Irish equivalent: *Shaothra' sé an bás go crua.*

Standard English version: *His last agony was prolonged* or *very painful.*

Anglo-Irish: *Faith, he gev a great shtagger.*

Irish equivalent: *M'anam gur thug sé seasamh uaidh.*

Standard English version: *His final illness was prolonged.*

Anglo-Irish: *'Tis well they earned him.*

Irish equivalent: *Is maith a cheanna' siad é.*

Standard English version: *They had a great deal of trouble tending him.*

Anglo-Irish: *'Tis little thinkin' he had this time lasht year he wouldn't be in it, the crayture.*

Irish equivalent: *Is beag a' smaointiú a bhí aige an t-am seo 'nura' nach mbeadh sé ann, an créatúr.*

Standard English version: *He little thought this time last year that he would be dead by now.*

Having done justice to that topic the two men turn to view the company. Soon they spy a strapping young fellow who is related to one of them. The other comments:

Anglo-Irish: *He's a fine splinther of a man, God bless 'im.*

Irish equivalent: *Balcaire breá fir is ea é, bail ó Dhia air.*

Standard English version: *He's a fine young fellow.*

Anglo-Irish: *The bate of 'im ishn't in it.*

Irish equivalent: *Níl a bhualadh ann.*

Standard English version: *He has no equal.*

Anglo-Irish: *He's the resht o' yeersel'.*

Irish equivalent: *'Sé 'n chuid eile dhaoibh fhéin é.*

Standard English version: *He's related to your family.*

Anglo-Irish: *He med a fine man with the lasht coupla years.*

Irish equivalent: *Rinne sé fear breá le cúpla bliain anuas.*

Standard English version: *He has developed into a fine man in the last few years.*

Anglo-Irish: *'Wondher he don't get married, an' what harm but there's no wan in the way on 'im.*

Irish equivalent: *Is mór an t-íonadh nach bpósann sé agus cén dochar ach níl aon duine sa mbealach air.*

Standard English version: *It's surprising that he doesn't get married seeing he has no encumbrance.*

Anglo-Irish: *Faith if there was a half-doshen in the way on 'im he'd be married long 'go.*

Irish equivalent: *M'anam dhá mbeadh leath-dhoisean sa mbealach air, bheadh sé póstaí fadó.*

Standard English version: *Indeed, if he had six to provide for he'd have married long since.* Alternatively: *If he had to provide for six he'd have married long since.*

One must question once again whether this last remark — however you may agree to frame it — is at all likely to occur outside an Irish context in the wider sense. The kind of emphatic paradox it expresses is certainly very characteristic of Ireland. Why is it then that one can supply a more or less Standard English version of it? We can answer this by pointing to the distinction between *performance* and *potential* in a language. We have supplied a potential form without guaranteeing that the Standard English speaker envisaged will in fact ever come to use it.

We may now review the text as a whole and compare notes on the essential characteristics of Anglo-Irish as illustrated above. Generally speaking, the material basis of the language, that is, words and grammatical forms, were very largely from English. Then consider the presentation: firstly pronunciation, and intonation, that is, the patterns of musical pitch in speech. You may agree that these two features were dominated by the Irish background as illustrated in the Irish sentences. Next we come to the difficult problem of phrase structure and here I shall be hard pressed to avoid the kind of explanation which obscures.

The European languages tend to express thought in the frame Subject + Predicate, for example, *God is just,* a proposition, by the way, of a kind basic to logic. In fact the development of logic as a discipline has been dominated by the possibility (not available in every language) of saying that X is Y. Another kind of European example is the Agent + Action type, for example *He broke his word.* English, Irish and Anglo-Irish have much phrase-making potential in common, as far as the material phrase patterns are concerned. These, however, are set in motion by a deeper structure namely, that of meaning. The allocation of phrase patterns to meanings is characteristically different in English and in Irish, and it does appear that Anglo-Irish follows Irish in this. An example may help: Anglo-Irish *There no word o' a lie in it* is rendered above by English *This is very true.* It is clear that the approach in each case is quite different and that the Anglo-Irish phrase structure would not be used in English in this case. But it *is* used in other cases, for example *There isn't a particle of humour in him.* So the same pattern exists but is applied to a different kind of context. Finally, it is clear that the Anglo-Irish phrase *There no word o' lie in it* runs parallel to the structure of the Irish phrase *Níl aon fhocal bréige ann,* which enables us to observe the act of creation at close quarters.

The speaker is in possession of the set of meanings and processes in his Irish sentence *Níl aon fhocal bréige ann* and he proceeds to carry out an Englishing operation upon it. What he does is to grasp at whatever English word material he can, and forge it into the patterns of the only language he knows. Sometimes the result, that is the Anglo-Irish, will throw light on the pattern of the underlying Irish, as when a native speaker compliments a girl's coiffure in such glowing terms as *Gerl! you have a hair!* representing the Irish sentence *A chailín, tá gruaig agat!* We can gather from the phrase *a hair* that in the Irish sentence, *gruaig* stands for 'a splendid head of hair'. In this way Irish base structures are brought to life as Anglo-Irish surface structures by way of English material. Consider, for instance, *he earned the death,* meaning 'he endured his death agony', *he's complainin'* meaning 'he's ill', *using* (food) for 'eating', *near himsel'* for 'stingy' or 'mean', *the resht of yeersel'* for 'a relation of your family'. Properly speaking, the phrase is the unit in all these cases, and the meaning of the single word is subordinate. Of special interest are sentences of transparent English word-material and patterning which have an unpredictable meaning. For example: *The mother ishn't too good to him* means 'His mother is not very well'. This sentence is generated from the same base as its Irish equivalent, *Níl an mháthair an-mha' aige.* Still another feature not to be missed is that in some cases up to three alternative Anglo-Irish phrases are generated to suit one particular Irish phrase: showing the creative spirit running free.

Such then is the meaning of Anglo-Irish in the first instance: language forming on the same base as corresponding Irish structures, with native intonation and pronunciation and a foraging for English materials. Would you call the material I have quoted here a kind of Irish or a kind of English? The view that it is a kind of Irish, in fact, English-Irish or Anglo-Irish derives from attention to the generative or creative aspect of language. The view that it is a kind of English depends on its utilisation of English materials and on the prospect of an eventual watering down of most if not all of the Irish elements in classic Anglo-Irish.

THE ANGLO-NORMANS AND THEIR ENGLISH DIALECT OF SOUTH-EAST WEXFORD

DIARMAID Ó MUIRITHE

After the Norman invasion of 1169 some of the adventurers who accompanied the expedition of Strongbow, Fitzstephen and Maurice Fitzgerald, settled in lands assigned to them in the South-East corner of Wexford, in a district now known as the baronies of Forth and Bargy. It may be assumed that some of these adventurers were infantry men in the service of Fitzstephen and Maurice de Prendergast, the two knights on whom Diarmaid Mac Murchadha conferred the baronies; and that there were Normans, Flemings, Welsh and English among them. During the century following the invasion their numbers were augmented by other followers of the Norman knights; and it is a simple historical fact that their descendants still inhabit the same corner of Wexford, a triangle of land between Wexford town, Bannow Bay and Carnsore Point, where names such as Parle, Codd, Strafford, Devereux, Lambert, Rossiter and Browne still predominate.

The early settlers did not meet with much resistance, and the little they did encounter was quickly and firmly dealt with. Within a century they seem to have settled down to the kind of life they knew in Pembrokeshire and Glamorganshire, masters of all they surveyed, rarely threatened by their Irish neighbours who had fled before them across Bannow Bay to the West and Forth mountain to the North. For centuries, the descendants of the first Anglo-Norman settlers lived in

comparative peace, and not until the Cromwellian
settlement took effect was their civilisation in real
danger. But even this plantation they survived, and
they retained, with singular fidelity, down to the middle
of the last century, many of their ancient, social and
domestic manners and customs, and a dialect of
English which, during its decline, they began to call
Yola — their word for old.

Before examining in some detail this old dialect of
Forth and Bargy, let me give you some specimens of it;
the first is from the oldest surviving folk-song in the
dialect, a hurling song, composed, it is thought, in the
first quarter of the eighteenth century. An old man tells
how his son Tomeen lost the match when he had the
goal at his mercy.

Forth

1
Na, now or neveare! w' cry't t' Tommeen,
Fan Cournug yate a rishp, an Treblere pit w'eeme.
A clugercheen gother: all, ing pile an ing heep,
Wourlok'd an anooree, lick lhuskes o' sheep.

2
T' brek up ee bathes h' had na poustee;
Tommeen was lous, an zo was ee baree.
Oore hart cam' t' oore mouth, an zo w' all ee green;
Th' hap, an ee ferde, an ee crie, was Tommeen.

3
Up caame ee ball, an a dap or a kewe
Wode zar; mot, all arkagh var ee barnaugh-blowe,
W' vengem too hard, he zunk ee commane,
An broughet ee stell, ing a emothee knaghane.

4
Th' ball want a cowlee, the gazb maate all rize;

Licke a mope an a mile, he gazt ing a mize;
Than stalket, an gandelt, wie o! an gridane.
Oore joys all ee-smort ing a emothee knaghane.

5

Ha-ho! be mee coshes, th'ast ee-pait it, co Joane;
Y' oure w' thee crookeen, an yie mee thee hoane.
He at nouth fade t'zey, llean vetch ee man,
Twish thee an Tommeen, an ee emothee Knaghane.

6

Come w' ouse, gosp Learry, theezil an Melchere;
Outh o'mee hoane ch'ull no part wi' Wathere.
Jaane got leigheen; shoo pleast aam all, fowe?
Shoo ya aam zim to doone, as w' be doone nowe:
Zo bless all oore frends, an God zpeed ee plowe.

The following is a Standard English translation by
General Vallency (c.1796):

1

Nay, now or never! we cry'd to Tommy,
When Cournug gave a stroke, and Treblere put with
   him, (helped him)
A crowd gathered up: all, in pile and in heap,
Tumbled on one-another, like flocks of sheep.

2

To break up the goal they had not power;
Tommy was open, and so was the goal.
Our hearts came to our mouth, and so with all in the
   green,
The chance, and the fear, and the cry, was Tommeen.

3

Up came the ball, and a tap or a shove
Would serve; but, all eager for the barnagh-stroke,
With venom too hard, he sunk his bat-club, (or bat)
And broke the handle in a pismire-hill.

4

The ball o-ershot the goal, the dust rose all about;
Like a fool in a mill, he looked in amazement;
Then stalked and wondered, with oh! and with grief.
Our joys are all smothered in a pismire-hill.

5

Hey-ho! by my conscience, you have paid it, quoth
    John;
Give over your crossness, and give me your hand.
He that knows what to say, mischief fetch the man,
Betwixt you and Tommy and the pismire-hill.

6

Come with us, gossip Larry, yourself and Miles;
Out of my hand I'll not part with Walter.
Joan set them a laughing, she pleased them all, how?
She gave them some to do, as we are doing now
    (drinking)
So bless all our friends, and God speed the plough.

The second specimen is the Lord's Prayer, a version
from Forth. It was collected towards the end of the last
century by William O'Neill, principal teacher of Ten
Acre school.

'Oure vaader fho yarth ing heaveene, ee-hallowet bee
t'naame. Thee kingdomw coome, thee weel be ee-
doane, as ing heaveene, zo eake an earthe. Yee ouze
todeie oure deilye breed, an varyee ouze our dettes, as
woúgh varyee our dettores; an leed ouze nat ing to
varsaakeen, mot varlouse ouze vrom evil. Vur theen
are ee kingdome an ee creft an ee lordlyeheed, ing
ayeheede, Amein.'

As Professor Bliss has already pointed out in his
essay, very little information about the English spoken
by the followers of the Norman war lords is available.
It is sometimes suggested that the English of South-
East Wexford may have been influenced by Flemish;

but it must be remembered that the Welsh colony of Flemings was, at the time of the conquest of Ireland, at least in its second generation, and was indeed, so eminently English that it was known as Little England Beyond Wales. Had Flemish influenced the English of the first settlers of the conquest to any great degree one would expect to find its influence in the vocabulary of the dialect of Forth and Bargy as it was in more recent times, but little trace of Flemish influence is discernible. (The Forth word moodher 'mother' is a relic of the early Flemish influence and it has found its way into the vocabulary of Irish poetry as múdar — cf. Dinneen's Irish-English Dictionary. The Forth word sthit 'filly' is related to the Middle Dutch Stotte 'mare'.) There are many words in modern English which begin with *F,* but in the dialect of Forth and Bargy, as in Flemish, with *V;* for instance, the words fire, finger and father, were in South-East Wexford, pronounced *vire, vinger, vather.* There was a similar change of *S* into *Z;* the Forth people said *zin, zay* and *zitch* instead of sun, say and such. But these peculiarities need not be attributed to a Flemish influence: they occur in nearly all the southern groups of the provincial dialects of England.

Forth and Bargy English contained many Irish words by Elizabeth's time and it is evident from Stanihurst's *Description of Irelande,* 1577, that the dialect differed widely from the speech of that queen's court:

'But of all other places, Weiseforde with the territorye bayed, and perclosed within the riuer called the Pill, was so quite estranged from Irishry, as if a traualler of the Irish (which was rare in those dayes) had picht his foote within the pile and spoken Irishe, the Weisefordians would commaunde hym forthwith to turne the other ende of his tongue, and speake Englishe, or else bring his trouchman with him. But in our dayes they haue so aquainted themselues with the

Irishe, as they haue made a mingle mangle, or gallamaulfrey of both the languages, and haue in such medley or checkerwyse so crabbedly iumbled them both togyther, as commonly the inhabitants of the meaner sort speake neyther good English nor good Irishe.

'There was of late dayes one of the Péeres of England sent to Weiseford as Commissioner, to decide the controuersies of that countrey, and hearing in affable wise the rude complaintes of the countrey clownes, he conceyued here and there, sometyme a worde other whyles a sentence. The noble man beyng very glad that vpon his first commyng to Ireland, he vnderstood so many wordes, told one of hys familiar frends, that he stoode in very great hope, to become shortly a well spoken man in the Irishe, supposing that the blunte people had pratled Irishe, all the while they iangled Englishe. Howbeit to this day, the dregs of the olde auncient Chaucer English, are kept as well there as in Fingall. As they terme a spider, an attercop, a wispe, a wad, a lumpe of bread, a pocket or a pucket, a Sillibuck, a copprouse, a faggot, a blease, or a blaze, for the short burning of it, as I iudge, a Phisition, a leache, a gappe, a sharde, a base court or quadrangle, a bawen, or rather, as I suppose, a barton: ye household or folkes, meany: Sharppe, kéene, estraunge, vncouth, easie, éeth oréefe, a dunghill, a mizen, as for the worde bater, that in English purporteth a lane, bearing to an high way, I take it for a méere Irishe worde, that crepte vnawares into the English, thorough the daily entercourse of the English and Irish inhabitants ...

'... And most commonly in words of two sillables, they giue the last the accent. As they say, Markeate, Baskeate, Gossoupe, Pussoate, Robart, Niclase, etc. which doubtlesse doth disbeautifie their Englishe aboue measure. And if they could be weaned from that corrupt custom, there is none that could dislyke of their English.'

In 1581, Sir Henry Wallop confirmed that 'to this day they generally speake oulde English'; and he was echoed a hundred years later by an anonymous correspondent of Sir William Petty, who wrote: 'they preserve their first language (old Saxon English), and almost only understand the same, unless elsewhere educated'. He added, significantly, I think: 'they seldom dispose of their children in marriage but unto natives, or such as will determine to reside in the barony'. This stay-at-home disposition was, no doubt, an important factor in the preservation of the old dialect; not alone did they not tolerate their children marrying outside the twin baronies, but they themselves rarely travelled outside them. There is a story in Shaw Mason's Parochial Survey of Ireland respecting a Forth woman, who happened, once in her life to go to the top of the plateau that separates Forth from the Irish territory to the North, and, she was so overwhelmed by the vast extent of the world which lay to the North of her own that she resolved never to venture on the appalling prospect any more. Another example of this mentality is to be found in a letter written by the historian Edmund Hore to the antiquarian Joseph Lloyd in 1875. Mr. Hore said that at a party given for the tenantry in the parish of Carne, by Sir Hugh Palliser, in 1821, one of the biggest attractions was the band of the old Wexford militia. 'The band', Mr. Hore recalled, 'was playing sprightly at a small distance, when a comfortable dressed woman of over 70 years, after gazing attentively for some time at the big drummer, sidled over to where we were standing, and with her gaze wholly absorbed in watching the big drummer, she exclaimed earnestly in a surprised tone: "Note, note, oh! Wiste lowaure thaare! Faade be dhicka fellowe lowaure a-doone, wi mucha cax avar im, an ercha dhime his striketh it, it zidth bow-wow. (I don't know, I don't know — oh, look below there! What is that fellow below there doing with the big cask before him, and every time he strikes it, it goes bow-wow.)" Though over 70 years of age, and living the mother of a large family on 4 or 5 acres in perfect contentment and comfort, she had never before seen a soldier, had never been in Wexford, 10 miles from Carne, nor further from her home than Killinick fair, 5 miles.'

By that time, 1821, the dialect was spoken only in Carne and Lady's Island, on the extreme elbow of Wexford, in the barony of Forth. It would appear that in the more westerly barony of Bargy, it gradually died out during the first half of the eighteenth century, though, around the time of the rebellion of '98, there were still many people around Kilmore Quay whose English was the butt of the more sophisticated citizens of Duncormack, on the western side of the barony of Bargy, five or six miles away. A mumming party from Duncormack went to Kilmore around the turn of the century, and, apparently, they didn't get the welcome they expected. A ballad composed by a Duncormack man pokes fun at the Kilmore English ...

In rank and fine order we marched to Kilmore,
Our only intention being Mass to procure,
But the messenger sent to us did say:
Fad didn'st thou coom t'ouz on zum other day?
Fad didn'st thou coom t'ouz phen w'ad sumthin t' yive?
But curse on the churls, tis at home we should live.

I would date the decline of the old dialect in the barony of Bargy from the time of Cromwell's incursion into Wexford, and the subsequent plantation. Apart from the slaughter in Wexford town, his soldiers raided deep into Forth and Bargy, destroying the seats of some of the principal families as well as levelling the great medieval shrine of Our Lady's Island; indictments for high treason had been laid against some of the principal families in 1642 and, unfortunately, the Act of Settlement, after the Restoration, did not empower them to recover their confiscated lands, then taken over by Cromwell's adverturers and soldiers. By all accounts, the Cromwellians got on reasonably well with the people of Forth and Bargy, but for the first time in centuries the peace of the baronies had been shattered, and a new kind of English was introduced in their midst.

One of the Cromwellians, Colonel Solomon Richards, who became governor of Wexford, left us an amusing account of the manners and customs of his neighbours in Forth. He noted that they had a strange custom, which they called *enteet*; and about this he wrote: 'About high noone, men and women, children and servants, naturally cease from labour, and go to rest for about an hour or two.' By the way, this *enteet* or noontide rest was observed in Forth until about 1900. In passing I might add that the old colonel had some startling things to say about how the Forth men treated their *mayen* or women. In describing the Forth mayen he says 'In one particular they excell all their sex in this kingdom: they so revere and honour the male sex, that to instance one particular only, if the master of the house be from home, his sonne, if any, or if none, than his chief servant present, though but a poor plough driver or cowboy, shall have the first mess of broath, or cut of meat, before the mistress or her female guests. This I know, but I have heard it affirmed that if there be no man or boy in the house, they will give the first bit to a cock or a dog, or any male creature.'

Mayen's lib, how are ye!

Before treating of the vocabulary of Yola, as they called it, and its folk songs, it is necessary to comment on the sounds of the dialect. About these we must take the word of our historian, Hore, who knew some of the last speakers of it. But by this time, the dialect had been influenced to a degree by ordinary Anglo-Irish, and Hore confessed that he was not sure about the pronunciation of some of the words found in the most important treasury of Forth and Bargy words, the glossary compiled by Jacob Poole towards the end of the eighteenth century and published in 1867. Neither Poole nor the schoolmaster, William O'Neill, who wrote down many folk songs and snatches of conversation from the old dialect, attempted phonetic transcriptions, and one can be confused by the variations in spelling found in their manuscripts. But both Hore and Poole's editor, Barnes, are nevertheless helpful; and the pronunciations of certain words that have survived into present-day speech, lend testimony to their accuracy. I quote from Dr. Barnes's introduction to his edition of Jacob Poole's glossary. Latter-day linguists would be amused at Barnes's terminology but I have chosen not to amend his notes.

'Mr. Hore writes that to give any idea of the Forth dialect one must speak slowly, "that the letter *a* has invariably the same sound, like *a* in father. Double *ee* sounds like *e* in me; and in most words of two syllables the long accent is placed on the last. To follow the English pronunciation deprives the dialect of its peculiarities."

We are not told what was the sound of the single *e* or *y* or long *i* nor of the diphthongs.

Eight sounds meet us in English grammar.

1. *ee* in meet.	5. *a* in father.
2. *e* long, Dorset.	6. *aw* in awe.
3. *a* in mate.	7. *o* in rope.
4. *ea* in earth, or the French *e* in le.	8. *oo* in food.

Besides diphthongs of pairs of these sounds.

The English 3rd sound long seems to have been in Forth the 5th sound written *aa,* or a sound written with *au* whether it was the 5th or 6th, as:

F.	E.	F.	E.
agyne	again	pyle	pail
amyne	amain	ryne	rain
brine	brain	mye	may
gryne	grain	mydhe	maid
gry	gray		

In other cases our *ai* are a diphthong *aay*, as

F.	E.	F.	E.
daaily	daily	laay	lay
faigh	faith	paay	pay
gaay	gay	waaite	wait
haail	hail		

answering to the Dorset *ai*,

faïth, gaÿ, haïl, paÿ, waït.

Our *and* of the 5th sound are often shown as *oan* of the 7th sound, or a diphthong of the 7th and a closer sound, sometimes written *one* or *oan*.

F.	E.	F.	E.
brone	brand	lone	land
broan		loan	
eelone	island	sthone	stand
eeloan		sthoan	
hone	hand	sthrone	strand
hoan		sthrone	

The 7th or 4th short-sounded *u* is often *ou*.

F.	E.	F.	E.
Chourch	Church	spourr	spur
chourle	churl	jooudge	judge
goooun	gun		

In some words *i* as

F.	E.	F.	E.
rin	run	risheen	rushing

Our long *i* diphthong of the 4th and 1st, as in *bride*, is mostly represented by *ee* or *ie* 1st.

F.	E.	F.	E.
griende	grind	neeght	night
heegh	high	ree	rye
neeghe	nigh	skee	sky
neen	nine	threeve	thrive
peepeare	piper		

Our diphthong *ou, ow*, has mostly become the pretty *eou* which we sometimes hear from London or Eastern County lips, as

F.	E.	F.	E.
greound	ground	pleough	plough
keow	cow	sneow	snow
meouth	mouth	steout	stout

A knowledge of these voicings of the speech will afford us some guidance for the correction of the unsettled spelling of the Glossary, by the bringing of an ill-grounded and almost single form of spelling to the better grounded form of the more usual shape.

The Forth shows a softening of the *f* into *v*, and the *s* into *z*.

It may have been in these clippings (articulations) that some readers may have deemed that they had found in the Forth dialect a mark of the Flemish; but it so happens that they are no more Flemish than they are West English, since, in Somerset and Dorset, they are yet strong, and in the Forth dialect they are coupled with another likeness to Wessex speech, the use of the affix to the past participle, which in Old English was written *y*, in Dorset is *a*, as the French *e* in *le*, and in Forth *ee*, as:

F.   ee-sarith uth in cooanes.
D.   a-saard out in (wooden) cans.
F.   platheares ee-zet in a row.
D.   platters a-zet in a row.
F.   Ho ro! mee cuck is ee-go.
D.   Ho roo! my cock is a-gone.

The likeness of the Forth and Dorset dialects may be shown by the numerals, as

F.	D.	F.	D.
oan	one	zeese,	zix
twye/twyne	two	zeven	zeven
dhree	dree	ayght	aight
voure	vower	neen	nine
veeve	vive	dhen	ten

Two consonants are sometimes parted by a voicing, as in the *vistes* and *postes* of Wessex,

halef	half	calef	calf

The more common plural ending is *es,* which, as Dr. Russell has observed, and as it seems from the measure of some of the verses, goes on to the singular word not only with its clipping *s,* as in English, but as a full-breath sound, as

"dugg-es an kaud-es", dogs and cats.

Some nouns, however, are found with the old Friesic-English plural ending *en,* as Ashen, ashes; Been, bees; Eeen, Ein, eyes; Fleen, fleas; Kyne, cows; Pizzen, peas; Shoone, shoes; Toan, toes; Tren, trees.

Another likeness of Forth to West English is the form of the pronoun *ich, I,* and its blending as *'ch* with verbs.

'Cham, for Ich aam, I am.
'Chas, for Ich waas, I was.
'Cha, for Ich ha, I have.
'Chull, for Ich wull, I will.
'Chood, for Ich would, I would.

In Devon we find,

'Cham, I am.
'Chave, I have.
'Chad, I had
'Chell, I will or shall.
'Chant, I won't or shan't.

"May be chell and may be chant", for, "It may be I shall, and it may be I shall not."

The definite article of the older Forth was *a* or *ee.*

There are a few markworthy cases of the softening of our *p* into a *b,* and of *t* into *d,* as in blenty, for plenty; boor, for poor; dell, for till; Beedher, for Peter, but this might have slipped in from the change of clipping in Irish. There is also a thickening of the *t* which might have come from the Irish.'

Well, these are some of the characteristics of the English of Forth and Bargy as it was spoken in the early nineteenth century. Let us turn now to its vocabulary. The first substantial collection of words from this district was made towards the end of the eighteenth century by General Vallency, a member of the Royal Irish Academy. The General claimed that he got his words from 'an old gentlewoman named Browne'; but I've seen a manuscript relating to Jacob Poole of Taghmon, which claims that the General borrowed his collection from Mr. Poole and published it without his permission. Be that as it may, Poole went on collecting, and before he died in 1827 he had gathered a most valuable collection of words from the two baronies. Here are a few examples:

Bederup, a band of reapers. In Blounts Law Dictionary of 1670 we find the word *bed-rip* ... a service which some tenants were anciently bound to perform, that is, to reap their landlord's corn at harvest.

Pauge-meale. Poole's editor, Barnes, says that the Pauge-meale was the harvest home, which is correct; but he doesn't tell us that the Paugh, from the Irish *póg,* a kiss, was the ceremonial kiss given to the woman of the house by the reaper who had cut the last handful of corn, which he then presented to her. *Meal* is derived from the Old English *mæl* 'time, season' so that pauge-meale is literally kissing time.

The Forth word for morning, *arich,* is related to the Old English *ærlice* 'early in the morning', while their *eatheet* and *eatheit,* evening, may represent an Old English *æthīd,* 'meal-time'.

Heal, the Forth word for health, is derived from Old

English *hǣlo. Met,* 'food' is derived from Old English *mete.* The dialect form *lereke, lerock, larock* 'lark', stems from Old English *lāwerce, lāferce.*

Kwingokee, churning, was one of numerous words the Forth and Bargy people borrowed from Irish. *Cuinneóg,* a churn. 'Wich ad wough beththter kwingokee or baagchoosee vursth?' (Which had we better churn or bake first?) is an expression Poole jotted down.

Ishe. Ishe meant 'ask'. Dinna ishe me a raison . . . don't ask me the reason.

Mayen was their word for women. Blessed y'art amang mayen . . . blessed art thou among women. Poole, unfortunately, did not give us the rest of the prayer. The singular, *mawen,* 'woman, wife', stemmed from Old English *mage.*

We might reasonably expect to find some remains indicating the Norman French connection. There are not many words of French origin in Poole's glossary, however. *Core,* the heart; *benisons,* blessings; *poustee,* power; *mire,* amazement; *hachee,* bad tempered; *lous,* praise . . . these are derived from French. There are, too, Norse words in Forth, such as *kaayle,* cabbage and *glaade* in the phrase 'to go to glaade', that is, to set (of the sun); but by and large the Norse influence is slight. Chaucer, of course, had most of these words, and in this connection, an anecdote related in *The Graphical and Historical Illustrator,* London 1834, is interesting.

'And here it may be related, as a singular fact, that the Rev. William Eastwood, Rector of Tacumshane, Barony of Forth, while amusing himself one day in his field with a volume of Chaucer, fancied some of the obsolete words which met his eye resembled those which also met his ear, as his workmen conversed together: he accordingly called them around him, and commenced reading a page or two of old Geoffrey aloud, to their great delight, as they well understood the most obscure expressions, and often explained them better than the glossarial aids of Dryden and Johnson.'

The schoolmaster, William O'Neill of Ten Acre in Forth, left us some interesting material too. The following conversation he — I assume it was he — jotted down in the pub of Paudeen Haaye in Tomhaggard. Haaye would be called Hayes elsewhere. Apparently one Dickeen Corishe was getting obstreperous, and Billeen Foughlaan (Coughlan) was doing his best to prevent him from raising a row. Mr. Corish spoke first: Dowst thou zee dhicka vellowe lewar? Hea's a kanat's faase apa'm. (Do you see that fellow beyond? He has a knave's face on him.) Chull goe ewer an geem oa knack. (I'll go over and give him a stroke.) To which the peacemaker, Mr. Foughlaan, replied: Faade ylth thee, thou sthouk? Sure, dhicka vellowe zyde nodthin ta thee. (What's wrong with you, you fool, sure that fellow said nothing to you.) Mr. Corish then said: Na mathar. Hea's a kanat's faase apa'm! (No matter, he has a knave's face on him!) To which Mr. Foughlaan said: Yith thou do na zitte deoune, chull brocke thee yola joule! (If you don't sit down, I'll break your old cheek!) Faade's dhicka vellowe zyen ore dooen t'thee? (What's that fellow saying or doing to you?) And that, apparently, saved the situation.

Among the schoolmaster's manuscripts I found a little song about the Maid of Rosslare, whoever she was ... EE Mydhe ov Rosslaare.

Cham goeen to tell thee oa taale at is drue,
Aar is in Rosslaare oa mydhe goude an drue,
Shoo wearth ing her hate oa ribbone at is blue
An shoo goeth to ee Faythe earcha deie too.

(I'm going to tell you a tale that is true,
There is in Rosslare a maid good and true,

She wears in her hat a ribbon that is blue
And she goes to the Faythe every day too.)

Ich loove ee mythe wee ee ribbone blue
At coomth to ee Faythe earche ariche too.
An chull her esholthe vor her ribbone blue,
Eh mythe at is leightzom, an well wytheen an drue.

(I love the maid with her ribbon of blue
That comes to the Faythe every morning too.
And I'll meet her for her ribbon blue,
The maid that is lightsome and goodlooking and true.)

I'll give you just one other example of this old
dialect. This too was preserved by the schoolmaster
O'Neill. It's called Zong o Dhree Yola Mythens ...
Song of three old maids. The three girls are lamenting
their fate: no man has come to take them to ilone vaar,
the island fair, associated with the great patron of Our
Lady's Island in the South of the barony of Forth.

Haar we be dhree yola mydhes
Fo naar had luck var to be brides
Fo no own kaars fadere betides
Dhree yola mythens.

(Here we are, three old maids,
Who never had luck to be brides,
Whom nobody cares what betides,
Three old maids.)

Wu canna baar to gow aveel
But zit at hime wi vlaxén wheel
An wish al fellows we a deel,
Poor yola mythens.

(We cannot bear to go abroad,
But sit at home by flaxen wheel
And wish all men with the devil,
Three old maids.)

We canna gow to Ilone vaar,
Thaar's no own al to taake us thaar
Or o a farrin gee's a shaar,
Poor yola mythens.

(We cannot go to the Island fair
There's no one at all to take us there,
Or of the fairing give us a share
Poor old maids.)

Wu'll go our wys to Chour Hill
An thaar zit down an yux our vill
An eachy tear ud shule a mill:
Poor yola mythens.

(We'll go our way to Chour Hill
And there sit down and sob our fill
And every tear would turn a mill,
Poor old maids.)

That song was probably composed in the late
eighteenth century; by the middle of the nineteenth
there were only two native speakers of the dialect left in
Forth. I have said that the Cromwellian settlement was
the first significant threat to the dialect; thereafter, the
standard English of the priests of the proscribed
Church must have had its influence too: Father
Devereux, who added to Luke Wadding's collection of
Christmas carols early in the eighteenth century, wrote
for the people of Forth and Bargy in standard English,
although he wrote one *ballad* in the Forth dialect. By
the mid eighteenth century, as I've said, the dialect was
not spoken to any great extent in Bargy; and the
decline spread. Dr. Russell of Maynooth, who
published a paper on the dialect in 1857 and said that
the youth of Forth had simply grown ashamed of the
ways of their elders and had accommodated
themselves to the customs by which they were
surrounded.

But it should not be thought that the people of these Wexford baronies lost all traces of their old tongue. They have retained to this day an extraordinary vocabulary, rich, and as one would imagine, a little odd. Hundreds of archaic words survive. A big fire is a breal (cf. Middle English *brule* 'to burn'). A parsnip is a neape (Old English *næp*). I have heard even young people use the old -n plural in the word ashen 'ashes'. There are, too, many words of obscure origin used in the baronies. A gorseejack is 'a young fellow, a bit of a pup' according to one of my informants. The words pulmare 'a strip of land in rundale' and harpleat 'snipe' may well be native Forth words also.

Alas, these old words are gradually falling into disuse, and I have a feeling that if I live long enough to return to Forth in thirty years time, I'll hear very few of the words I've collected over the years in the place. But that's another story.

THE DIALECTS OF ULSTER

G. B. ADAMS

If you draw two parallel lines across the map, one from Bundoran to Dundalk and the other from Drogheda to Sligo, you will mark off a zone of transition between southern and northern Hiberno-English. South of that zone there is a good deal of homogeneity within southern Hiberno-English, which has spread outwards from its base area in the seven counties of Dublin, Wicklow, Wexford, Carlow, Kildare, Leix and Offaly into what were formerly and till fairly recently Gaeltacht areas. North of the transitional zone there is much less homogeneity, for reasons which we will come to later: the point I want to make here is that in the course of the eighteenth and nineteenth centuries English spread into this zone from two directions. It spread northwards from the Pale towards Ulster, and it spread southwards from central Ulster towards this border area, so that within the zone of transition one finds a whole series of boundary lines between different phonological and lexical features that mark the transition from southern to northern Hiberno-English.

Now, within the total area of the northern counties the linguistic position is rather more complex than it is south of this border zone. Whereas southern Hiberno-English had a single origin in the English of England, the speech of the northern area had a double origin in which this was only one source, and not by any means the most important one. A more widespread source was Lowland Scots, and it must be remembered that in the early seventeenth century, when both forms of the English language, using that term in its wider sense, were introduced into the north of Ireland, English in the narrower sense and Scots had almost reached the stage of being separate languages.

After three centuries of political separation, England and Scotland had both developed standard language forms on the basis of the dialects of the London region and of the Edinburgh region. Had the two countries not been united, it is fairly certain that their languages would have continued to diverge, rather as Danish and Swedish diverged in Scandinavia. But as a result of the union of Scotland and England under one king in 1603 and one parliament in 1707, their two forms of language converged again and a situation developed not unlike that which existed between Denmark and Norway for many centuries, where the literary and official language of Norway was really Danish pronounced with a Norwegian accent. In the same way during the eighteenth century English became the standard and official language of Scotland, though there it was pronounced with a Scots accent. At the time when the Scots settled in great numbers in Ulster, however, the separation of English and Scots was a reality.

Now, it has been said that there were about 150,000 Scottish settlers in Ulster and about 20,000 English. It must be remembered that amongst the Scots a certain number were Gaelic-speakers, not only from the Highlands but also from western Galloway which at that time was still partly Gaelic-speaking, so we could perhaps say that the Scots outnumbered the English by about six to one. There was a difference, however, between the north-eastern coastal areas of Ulster, where the Scots settled in great numbers with very few English settlers among them, and the Plantation areas of inner Ulster where the Scots were less numerous and they and the English intermingled. This led to a reduction in the number of distinctively Scottish features that survived and in the greater part of Ulster today we find various forms of generalised northern Hiberno-English whose source is a mixture of English dialects in the narrower sense and of Lowland Scots. In some parts the bulk of the population is probably derived from native-speakers of this mixture of dialects. In other areas it has spread into places where Irish formerly predominated; but overall there has been widespread generalisation of northern Hiberno-English.

There is, however, a belt of territory in which, at least among the rural population though to a diminished extent among the urban population, a pure Scots dialect is still spoken. This dialect is possibly of a somewhat more archaic type than that which is now spoken in Scotland itself. The largest area within this belt of territory begins at Whitehead and its boundary line runs south-westwards, about a mile back from the coast, just north of Glengormley down to Dundrod. Then it turns north to the east of Antrim and swings round north of Antrim to the Long Mountain. It goes up the Long Mountain to just south of Rasharkin and then swings north-west across the Lower Bann near Kilrea and continues in a more or less straight line to the mouth of the River Roe on the shores of Lough Foyle. Within this north-eastern area there is one major exception to the statement that it is a Scots-speaking area. On Rathlin Island and in the north-eastern glens from Ballycastle round by Armoy and Cargan to just north of Carnlough one finds again the generalised northern Hiberno-English which in this area has replaced Irish in quite recent times.

The second part of this belt is a continuation of the first on the other side of Belfast Lough. It begins at Groomsport and, running along the escarpment of the Holywood Hills and across the Dundonald gap to Gilnahirk, continues south-westwards through

Carryduff and Boardmills, where its boundary line gradually swings round to run eastwards to Strangford Lough just north of Killyleagh. It begins again at the Saltwater Bridge north of Ardkeen in the Ards peninsula and runs across this to Cloghy. The third portion of the Ulster Scots area is in east Donegal. Its boundary begins a mile or two north of Muff and runs across to Lough Swilly, including Inch Island, then across the Fanad peninsula through Carrowkeel, Milford, Termon and round by a point about half-way eastwards to the Foyle near Clonleigh. This is the Laggan area where many Irish-speakers from north-west Donegal went as young folk 'to lift the Scotch', as they said, before starting off on seasonal migration to Scotland itself, with the result that it was a fairly scotticised form of English that later spread into north Donegal.

It is interesting that this semi-circle running from Cloghy, near the southern end of the Ards peninsula, round the eastern and northern coasts into east Donegal links up almost continuously with the surviving Gaeltacht area in West Donegal. The only exceptions north of this composite belt where generalised northern Hiberno-English has taken root are in the north-eastern glens of Antrim, already mentioned, and in the Inishowen peninsula. In the areas south of this mainly coastal belt there were, of course, places where the Scots were numerous in the seventeenth century, especially around Cookstown, in parts of south Down, in a narrow belt across the middle of Armagh, in parts of Monaghan and east Fermanagh, around Derrygonnelly and in south Fermanagh. But they were much less numerous here and were not reinforced by continuous contact with Scotland, with the result that although individual features of Scots origin survive, one does not find an Ulster Scots dialect in the way that one does in the north-eastern crescent.

Now, just to show what this dialect is like I would
like to quote a poem I collected many years ago from a
Larne bus driver, one of whose colleagues nicknamed
True-Blue, had hit a pig and killed it on the road from
Raloo to Larne:

T'ue B'ue was comin fae Raloo
The day he kalt McCaamont's soo.
He hut her hard atween the een
The cleanest clout ye ever seen.
Then doon she went wuthoot a squeal,
The oul coalie-dug was at harr heel.
He turned aboot an lot a yell
An ann the gate he run like hell.
McCaamont heerd the bloomin fuss,
Looked ower the waa an saa the bus.
Then oot he come tae hae a squaat,
Sez he 'Boy, whut made you dae thaat?'
'Weel' T'ue B'ue sez 'Maan, can't ye see
Your pagg run oot ann front o me,
For on ma brake an clutch A stid
But thaat aa proved tae be nae gid.'
Then the pleece come up fae oot the toon
An they measured the road baith up an doon.
The yann pleecemaan tae the ather sez
'No more on this roadside she'll graze'
The owner's sann, A heerd a whud,
Allood the soo was worth fafteen quud;
But his brather sez 'You're maakin fun,
Thaat soo was weel worth tharty pun.'
So the soo was tuck tae the abbatoar
An the butchers come fae the Lord knows whaur
Each hopin there wuthin his sowl
Tae baay the oul soo thaat was felt stane-coul.
Weel, the butcher-maan thaat boght the soo,
He wundhered whut was best tae do,
For the clout she gaut, the soo t'wud spoil;
'Ah, whut dazznae dae tae fraay' sez he

'T'wull mebbe dae tae boil.'
So he made harr anntae sausage-meat,
Harr heed, harr lugs, an aa harr feet.
Whut wudnae gae anntae sausage-meat,
He made it anntae veal.
A'll tell ye hoo he endit up,
He only loast the squeal.

From about 1770 onwards this dialect was cultivated to a considerable extent by local poets who flourished mainly in mid Antrim, east Antrim and north Down. They were not just imitating Robert Burns but belonged to a tradition going back to Alan Ramsay and beyond in Scotland. Their greatest period of activity was roughly the century between 1770 and 1870, but the tradition has lingered on in County Antrim to some extent even to the present day.

You will have noticed some of the Scots phonological features belonging to this dialect, for example the *gh* which we still write is fully pronounced in words like *boght, thoght, doghter, laagh, cogh, enyugh,* whereas in ordinary northern Hiberno-English this is confined to dialect words of Northumbrian origin and to loanwords from Irish. Another feature is the *ae*-sound instead of *o* in *baith* for *both, hame* for *home, stane* for *stone.* When the original vowel was in contact with *w* the result is *aa,* as *blaa* for *blow.* Then there is the *oo* sound for standard English *ow,* as in *soo* for *sow, hoose* for *house, toon* for *town,* while on the other hand *ow* occurs often where standard English has *o* or other vowels, as in *grou* for *grow* and *yow* for *ewe.* The Ulster *oo* sound among speakers of all kinds, whether of local dialect or of the regional standard, is a much more advanced sound than in other parts of these islands, while at the same time the long *o* is a very close sound. I remember being on holiday in Kerry one time and on arrival at the hotel I noticed there was no soap at the basin so I asked the bedroom-girl for some.

After some hesitation and a repeat of my request she said 'If you wait now for half an hour dhey'll be serving soup in the dining-room.' What was *soap*/sɔ:p/ and *soup*/su:p/ to her was /sop/ and /süp/ to me. My *soap* was close enough in sound to her *soup* for confusion to arise.

In Ulster Scots dialect the *oo*-sound is often unrounded to *ae* or *i* according as it is long or short, for example *dae gid* for *do good*, but the short sound does not fall together with the original short *i*, because this is shifted to short *a*, while original short *a* in turn is treated as a somewhat lengthened back vowel. Thus in place of *loom, limb, lamb* one hears *lim, lamm, laam*, and in place of *rock* and *pot* one hears *rauk* and *paut*. I remember being in the changing-room of my tennis club once and hearing one fellow saying to another 'I'm very fat.' I looked round at him and saw that he wasn't fat at all; he was a wee skinny fellow; you couldn't have seen him behind a tram-ticket. Then I realised he was a member of a visiting team from Ballymena and what he had really said was 'A'm very fatt (f-i-t). If he had really meant what I thought he said, he would have said 'A'm very faat.' Words that sound alike in standard English are often different in this dialect, for example the adverb *well* is *weel,* but the *well* you get water out of is a *waal,* while a *wall* is a *waa,* with loss of final *l*.

When we turn to those areas where the main source of northern Hiberno-English was the speech of various regions of England, we find that there was less homogeneity of origin among the English than among the Scots in Ulster. There were people from East Anglia and Northampton in north Armagh, parts of east Donegal and in north Fermanagh; the London form of their East Midland dialect was the source a couple of centuries earlier of standard English and must have been spoken in some form by most of the London companies' settlers in Londonderry. Equally numerous, perhaps, though more concentrated, were people from Devonshire and west Somerset who settled around the Belfast area and in south antrim and south-east Tyrone. More numerous still were those who came from the southern part of the West Midland dialect area, that is from Warwickshire, Staffordshire and Shropshire and to some extent the surrounding counties. They settled in south Antrim, north-west Down, across north Armagh in much greater numbers than the East Anglians, in central Tyrone around Omagh, in parts of south Tyrone and east Fermanagh, and around Limavady and Bellaghy. The remaining area which gave settlers in some numbers to Ulster was the northern West Midland dialect area of Lancashire, Cheshire and south-west Yorkshire, who settled mainly in the Lagan valley from Belfast up to Moira and to some extent around Ballynahinch.

Now, one thing about these English settlers is that speakers of different English dialects were mixed with each other and in many places with Scots. One result of this is that the more distinctive features of their various English dialects have disappeared. For example, people from Devonshire and west Somerset must have had that well-known Wessex feature of pronouncing *z* for *s* and *v* for *f* at the beginning of many words, as *zide* and *zummer* for *side* and *summer,* and *volk* for *folk,* but this has not survived in any part of Ulster. The fact that the English dialects would have been nearer to standard English than was the case with the Scots dialects led to a greater tendency for speech to be assimilated to a regional form of standard English.

This regional form, of course, was standard English as it was spoken in the later seventeenth century when it had not yet developed some of the features that characterise the so-called RP pronunciation of standard English in England today. Nevertheless some distinctively English dialect features have survived, like the West Midland *ow* for *o* before *l* plus a consonant in *ould, cowld, boul* for *old, cold, bowl.* Curiously enough, this sound also occurs before *ld* in Ulster Scots, as in the case of certain areas in Scotland itself, such as Easter Ross and South Kintyre which were settled by Scots Lowlanders at the same time as Ulster, whereas Scots in general has *auld* and *cauld.*

When we turn from sounds to vocabulary we find that the English of Ulster has preserved many older words that have gone out of use in England. It has been said that more of Shakespeare's words are still used in Armagh than in present-day Warwickshire itself. We still use the word *thole,* 'to put up with', a word of Old English origin now generally obsolete. Some dialect words are recognised as such but many are used in the ordinary way by speakers of the regional standard of northern Hiberno-English without realising that they are dialect words till they meet a speaker from some other region who does not know them. If you are eating an orange and break it up into its natural divisions, each one of these is called a *lith.* It is only in recent years that I have discovered that English people do not know this, though the Scots do. In some northern dialect areas of England this word is used to denote a group of warp threads in the loom, while in some mining areas *lith* denotes a seam of coal, but in the south of England it is quite obsolete. Regarding Scots items in the vocabulary which are used not only in dialect but often in the regional standard vocabulary, they are generally found in the south-western dialects of Galloway and Strathclyde. For example, we have *wean* for 'child', whereas the more easterly Scots dialects have *bairn*; I doubt if this occurs in Ulster at all. Some Scots words are of Gaelic origin and this, of course, complicates the whole question of Gaelic loanwords in Ulster English. We have words that have come direct from Irish, especially in the western part of the province, words that passed from Scottish Gaelic into some form of Ulster English in Ulster itself and words that had entered Lowland Scots from Gaelic before the former was brought to Ulster at all. In many cases these different strata of loanwords can be distinguished by their phonology. Once established some of these loanwords have spread, while others are confined to small areas.

Let's take another example of the Ulster Scots dialect, a story I recorded some years ago from Cullybackey in west Antrim. You must imagine three old fellows talking together in a bachelor farmhouse and their conversation runs like this:

'Jammie, you're an oul baachelor, A hear. It's a wundher ye navver married.'

'Oh you're aa wraang there, Joahn, A'm no an oul baachelor, A'm a weeda-maan. Aye, ma wife deed wheen we were jist a year married, wheen harr waen was boarn.

'Weel, Jammie, A'm soary tae hear thaat, but it's a wundher ye navver married again.'

'Weel, Joahn, it's no but A haad a notion o it a lauk o times. There was a wee laass o Joe Rainey's A haad a terrible notion o for a while but A was scarred she wud be crauss. A was aye gey an feered o gettin a crauss yann, an A saa harr puttin baak harr ears at harr maa a wheen o times, so aai shied aaf. Onywey harr ain yanns thoght aai was a batt scuffed, bein merried afore.'

'But was there nae ather hazzies ann Bellyclose ann need o a maan?'

'Aye, aye, Joahn, ye haad yann there the day helpin ye tae malk the kaay, but it wasnae yann maan she waantit ann harr young days; it was a dazzen. Aff aai haad been harr fether A wud hae whaamled harr. She wud taak a maan yatt at saxty but aai dannae waant tae start brangin up a femly noo.'

'Naebiddy else ye thoght aboot, Jammie? Surely the wornae aa baad?'

'Weel, A haad ma ee on Taam Sampson's doghter, Eggie, yannst. Mine ye, a taght wee hazzie she was then. It's no tae luck at harr noo, a kine o a baaghel wae a laaghter like thaun roon harr. Weel, efter thankin it ower a wheen o years A made it up wae Raab — ma croanyie sattin ower there on the haab — tae go an aaks harr fether. A was gey an scarred, for Taam was doatin aboot laan, an me wae ma wee saiven acres wasnae very much tae waste a doghter on. Onyway Raab here thoght thaat it wud be betther tae saafen Taam wae a dhraap o whusky — ye know Raab likes tae get saafened thaat way hassel. Weel, yann Seturday naght A caad for Raab tae go wae me — an A daddnae forget the whusky — but wheen A caad a coo was caavin, so he toul me tae go on. He was laanger ann the leg nor me and he wud owertaak me. Wheen aai got ower thaun bautom o yours an throo the whuns, A made for the slaap whaur the kaay staans waitin tae be broght ann tae be malked. The next thang A knowed ma yann fit slapped ann behann the ather yann an doon A went aan ma groof ann the coo shairn. Thaat wasnae aa. Wheen A spraaghled aboot traayin tae get up shae nor fit cud A putt undher me. A haad staived me aankle. At laast A gaut on ma baakside an airsed ower tae A gaut a houl o yann o thaun pailin posts forninst the lannt daam. A was there aboot an oor an A was chaakin wae the coul, an claarried wae coo dung fae heel tae thraaple. A thoght Raab wud navver come. At laast A hard his wheeple ann the whuns, an A was gey an gled tae see his bagg feet as he lept ower the dike. He jist lucked at me an he says:

'"Jammie, is thaat you?" Sez aai:

'"Whaa dae ye thank it wud be? A hae broke ma leg."

'"Naw," sez he, "is the whusky aa raght?"

'Then he gaut his airse agann the stump o a tree an pulled oot his pipe. He laghtit a maatch. It blowed oot.

Then he laghtit anather yann an hel it ower naxt maay
face.

‘ "Jammie," sez he, "there's mair coo dung ann yer
ear than wud grou a gid taap o praetas." A was gey an
aangry at him. Wheen he smoked a while he says:
"Kin ye maak the lenth o Taam's?"

‘ "A caan naut," sez aai, "a waant tae get away
baak hame."

‘At laast Raab got me auxtered tae thaun stile o
yours an we sut doon on it an drunk the whusky, Mine
ye, A was quare an gled tae get anntae ma settle bed
thaat naght.’

‘Thaat was terrible, Jammie. But whut aboot Eggie?
Dadd ye no go baak again aboot harr?’

‘Naw 'deed, Joahn, A navver bauthered.’

Well, that is one example of Ulster Scots dialect.
One of the things I think should be said is that when
people from other parts of Ireland try to reproduce
northern speech they all too often fail to distinguish
between Ulster Scots and Ulster English in the
narrower sense, and produce curious combinations
that do not actually occur in practice. It may perhaps
help to make clear the difference between these
different types of northern speech if I take a few lines
of a well-known poem by W. F. Marshall, entitled *Me
and me Da*. Some of you probably know it. It begins:

I'm livin in Drumlister,
An I'm gettin very oul;
I have to wear an Indian bag
To save me from the coul.
The deil a man in this townlan'
Was claner raired nor me,
But I'm livin in Drumlister
In clabber to the knee.

There is no need to quote the whole poem. He
thought he would improve his lot by taking a wife and

the original poem in County Tyrone dialect as
Marshall wrote it goes on as follows:

Well, I know two I thought would do,
But still I had me fears,
So I kiffled baack an forrit
Between the two for years.

   Transposed into County Antrim dialect this would
be:

Weel, A know twaa A thoght wud dae,
But stal A haad ma fears,
Sae A kaffled beck an faurit
Atween the twaa for years.

   Unfortunately he kiffled a bit too long. Margit got a
man, a fellow from Mullaslin married her and left him
'jist the waan'. He laments the day she got married in
the following lines:

I mind the day she went away,
I hid wan strucken hour,
An cursed the wasp from Cullentra
That made me da so sour.
But cryin cures no trouble,
To Bridget I went baack
An faced her for it that night week,
Beside hor own toarf-staack.

   Transposed into County Antrim dialect this would
be:

A mine the day she went awaa,
A hud yann strucken oor,
An cursed the waasp fae Cullentraa
Thaat made ma daa sae soor.
But craayin cures nae trabble,
Tae Bridget A went beck
An faced harr for it thaat naght week,
Beside harr ain turf-steck.

He got the shock of his life when she wouldn't have him and the poem ends with the sad reflection that he's

... dyin in Drumlister,
In clabber to the knees.

These lines, with their translation from one dialect to another, are examples of the contrasting types of English that one may find in the north of Ireland. There are parts of the north-east where many people are bilingual in two varieties of English, just as they may be bilingual in Irish and English in parts of the south and west. They use one variety, Ulster Scots, among themselves and another variety, an approximation to the regional standard, in talking to strangers. I remember getting petrol one time at a garage a couple of miles from Glengormley, a northern suburb of Belfast. The man serving me was talking to a local with a bicycle, and I noticed that he said *doon* to him for *d-o-w-n*, whereas he said *down* to me. Such is the variety of English spoken in the north of Ireland.

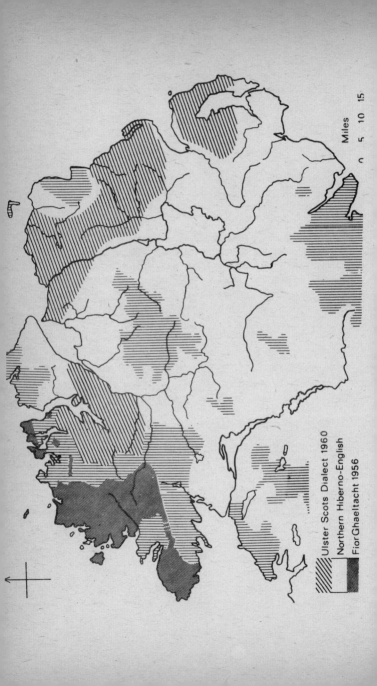

Ulster Scots Dialect 1960

Northern Hiberno-English

Fíor Ghaeltacht 1956

Miles
0   5   10   15

THE DOMINANCE OF THE ENGLISH LANGUAGE IN THE NINETEENTH CENTURY

SEÁN DE FRÉINE

To find the origins of the great language shift which took place in Ireland in the nineteenth century it is necessary to go back to the beginning of the previous century. The earliest reliable references to a concerted movement from the Irish language to English date from shortly after the year 1700. During the previous centuries, once the native culture had recovered from the initial shock of the Anglo-Norman invasion, the Irish language showed itself to be both tenacious and resilient. Even in the seventeenth century, which was so disastrous from the Irish point of view, the language held its own outside the areas of the Plantation of Ulster. All through that century, which began with the defeat of Kinsale in 1601, and which experienced the Cromwellian invasion and plantation, Irish continued to be spoken, not merely by the mass of the common people, but by people of education, property and influence. A noteworthy feature of that time is the prevalence of Irish in the heartland of the Pale. One reason for this was the increasing pressures of the Reformation which accentuated an awareness of a common Irishness among the old English-speaking populace of the country.

Evidence of this development is to be seen in the establishment of the Irish college at Douai in 1594. This college was founded by Father Christopher Cusack, grandson of a former Lord Chancellor, as an instrument of the Counter-Reformation. It provided

education for the sons of the principal families of the
Pale. Its extensive curriculum included learning and
speaking Irish. In the year 1600 an English agent
reported on the college to London: 'They all speak
Irish and they pray for O'Neill.'

Irish seems also to have become common among
the ordinary people to within a short distance of
Dublin. Writing to Father Luke Wadding in 1629
about certain newly-ordained priests who were natives
of the city, Archbishop Thomas Fleming complained
that for want of Irish they were unable to minister
outside the city, and so 'must be idle with their parents,
to their great charge and grief'. That the language
made inroads into Fingal appears from a reference to
the secret ministrations of a Capuchin friar in 1650, in
the vicinity of Swords in north County Dublin, where
he preached in Irish. In the same year Patrick
Sarsfield, Earl of Lucan, was born and brought up
with Irish as well as English in what is now virtually a
suburb of Dublin city.

Sarsfield's departure from Ireland in 1692 with his
army of 11,000 men, and the subsequent Williamite
confiscations, brought about a new set of linguistic
circumstances. By 1713 Irish had receded again from
Fingal, according to the *Introduction to the Irish
Language* by Father Francis Walsh. He refers to
English as being 'now the most common and most
prevailing language with the learned and unlearned of
our country', and he apologises for his inadequacies by
saying 'A perfect Irish grammar ought not to be
expected from me, and be it as imperfect or as much
deficient as you please, it is but reasonable to think it
enough, as coming from a Fingallian.' Shortly after this
another writer living in Dublin, Tadhg Ó Neachtain,
laments the fact that there are no nobles of the Gaelic
race who do not now repudiate their language. The few
of them who still survived adopted English in order to
be as unobtrusive as possible in a hostile environment.

Typical of this new development was Richard Hennessy, son of a well-to-do Catholic family who later gained fame as French brandy distillers. Hennessy was born near Killavullen in County Cork in 1720 and went to France in 1740. Only then, when he joined the Irish Brigade, did he learn to speak Irish.

As the century progressed, a new native Irish urban populace emerged, who saw in English the key to their material well-being. Forbidden by law to own land, these people turned quite successfully to commerce and other activities which the law did not prohibit to them. By the end of the century they were well established as a class who were town-born and-bred. English was their language, to such an extent that as early as 1752 proposals were made in Dublin to found a club because 'Irish, the mother tongue of this nation, has long been neglected and discouraged ... and the natives find themselves alone among the natives of the earth ignorant for the most part of the language of their fathers.' Almost a quarter of a century later the English traveller, Richard Twiss, observed in 1776 that Irish was still spoken by most of the common sort, but by few of the better class of people.

Apart from this development, however, the language situation at the end of the eighteenth century was not all that different geographically from what it was in the year 1700. There was a certain amount of give and take in the territories occupied by the two languages. English gains in Leinster were countered by Irish gains in the plantation areas of Ulster, parts of which were ravaged by Presbyterian emigration in the eighteenth century. In most of the towns the emergence of an English-speaking Catholic class was matched by the growth of a much larger population of urban poor whose first language was Irish.

It is difficult at this remove in time to appreciate the complexity of the linguistic situation about the year 1800. The very success of the English language in extending its sway in the course of the nineteenth century tends to mask the reality of the situation. In the first place, there were not two, but six, distinct speech communities in the country. Apart from the two principal languages, Irish and English, the old dialect of Yola might still be heard in the baronies of Bargy and Forth in County Wexford. French and German-speaking communities, some of them established over a hundred years before, were still to be found: French at Portarlington, Lisburn, Dublin and other places; German at Gracehill near Ballymena, and at places in Tipperary and Limerick. The sixth speech community was that of Lallans, or Lowland Scotch, which was extensive in many parts of the north. It was a very pure dialect of Scottish, and we are told by various observers that it was almost unintelligible to strangers.

Trying to piece together the shattered jigsaw which comprised the language map of Ireland about the year 1800 is not an easy task. Many of the pieces have been lost. Statistics are unreliable, prejudiced, or entirely lacking. We may, however, get an idea of what the picture was like by emulating the example of all experienced jigsaw addicts. We will begin by trying to fill in the outline of the puzzle. For us, that means following the coastline. Fortunately, we can put these pieces together with a fair degree of reliability.

Let us begin where the story of the English language in Ireland may be said to have begun — at Hook Head in County Wexford. Here the first Normans landed in the year 1169. In 1800 this part of County Wexford was Irish speaking. From Bannow Bay nearby to the town of Wexford the Normans left a more permanent trace — the Yola dialect. From Wexford town northwards to Drogheda the coast was English-speaking, apart possibly from some Irish in the vicinity of Gorey and Arklow. From Drogheda to the shores of Strangford Lough the Irish language predominated.

From Strangford Lough to Belfast the speech was
Lowland Scotch. From Belfast to Larne English again
took over. From Larne to Glenarm Scotch recurred.
From Glenarm to Ballycastle we find an Irish-speaking
enclave, physically isolated from the other Irish areas
in the country, but in close contact with the Gaelic-
speaking territories of Islay, Kintyre and Arran in
Scotland. From Ballycastle to Derry the coast was
strongly Scotch. The remaining three-quarters of the
coastline, from Derry north by Inishowen and round
by the west coasts of Donegal, Connacht and Munster
and back to Hook Head was practically all Irish-
speaking.

Inland, it is more difficult to put the picture together.
It is possible, however, to begin with some certainties.
North County Dublin was English-speaking, only
traces of the old Fingallian dialect (which had affinities
with Yola) remaining in the common speech. South of
Dublin, most of County Wicklow had become English-
speaking since 1750, probably because it had been
thinly populated, was heavily settled by the eighteenth-
century ascendancy, and because its remotest glens
had experienced considerable mining activity. English
also predominated in mid-Wexford, and probably
along the north Wexford coast. Moving inland, we find
English dominant by the year 1800 in Counties
Kildare and Carlow. Here too the decline had begun
about 1750. The anglicisation produced by substantial
plantation seems here to have been augmented by a
very efficient programme of education provided in all
the Catholic chapels of the Diocese of Kildare and
Leighlin by the Confraternity of Christian Doctrine.

Further inland, in Counties Laois and Offaly,
the situation is less clear, and contradictory statements are made about the language position there.
The truth probably lies midway between extremes, and
it would seem that more Irish was known in those parts
than in the counties further to the east, but that much

more English was used in business and publicly than in
Connacht or Munster. The north Leinster counties of
Louth, Meath, Westmeath and Longford were still
mainly Irish-speaking. So too was County Kilkenny —
the southern half of the county being described as 'as
Irish as any place in Connacht'. In north Wexford and
the adjoining portions of Carlow, Irish was also
spoken. In Ferns it continued to be used in Catholic
sermons until 1810. In 1820 the Reverend John Feeley,
a Methodist convert from Catholicism and a native of
County Carlow, was preaching regularly in Irish in
Bunclody. There are quite a few other references to
Wexford Irish dating from that period.

Although English was predominant in much of
south Leinster, Irish was still recent enough to be close
to the surface of what appeared to be an English-
speaking countryside. Methodist missionary activity in
the area demonstrates this. Early in the century, the
Methodist Church appointed preachers to traverse the
country in pairs — to preach in Irish and English.
Samuel Alcorn and James Bell were appointed for the
province of Leinster. They preached throughout their
area on horseback, 'in the streets, on the Lord's Day,
and at markets and fairs'. Mr. Bell preached with
fervour, we are told, in Irish. These two men
commenced their mission on the public street in Naas,
in 1806, where, to the east, a strip of Irish seems to
have survived along the western flanks of the Wicklow
Mountains, extending eastwards into the mountain
valleys of Glenasmole and Glencullen in County
Dublin. Other Irish-speaking Methodist missionaries
preached in Leinster too: James M'Quigg in Kilkenny
and Laois; Charles Graham in Westmeath, Longford,
and Offaly; and, practically everywhere, the
indefatigable and colourful Gideon Ouseley, who
earned for himself the popular sobriquet of *Síoda na
bhFear*.

Beyond the Shannon, Connacht was virtually

entirely Irish-speaking in 1800. English was so little known among the mass of the people that the gentry and well-to-do classes had to acquire it if they wanted to communicate with their servants and tenants. In 1823 Irish was said to be almost exclusively the language of Galway city, the only city and the most important centre of commerce in the province.

The Irish language was also general throughout the province of Munster, but English was much more widely known than in Connacht, particularly in Tipperary.

In Ulster the religious divide between Roman Catholic, Church of Ireland, and Presbyterian approximated to the linguistic divisions of Irish, English and Lowland Scotch. There were, however, some divergences from this: there were Catholics who knew no Irish, and there were Church of Ireland folk and Presbyterians in Counties Donegal, Antrim and Down, who were Irish-speaking.

English was, of course, the language of the upper classes in all the cities and towns. But Irish speakers were also to be found in most towns, excluding Wexford town, the towns of Counties Wicklow, Kildare and Dublin, and the towns of East Ulster. These urban Irish-speakers were generally poor and uneducated, but their numbers could be appreciable. James McQuige said in 1818 that he had seen the court in Londonderry idle for several hours for want of an interpreter. In the same city, in 1837, an enthusiastic English evangelist exclaimed: 'Yesterday I sallied through Butcher's Gate ... but did not go far. That quarter, called the Bogside, is the counterpart of our London St Giles and inhabited by a most uncivilised population. I did not explore it but longed for the time and opportunity to make a sally through that gate ... seconded by a party of Irish scripture readers.' In Belfast the small Catholic population at the start of the nineteenth century was soon to be

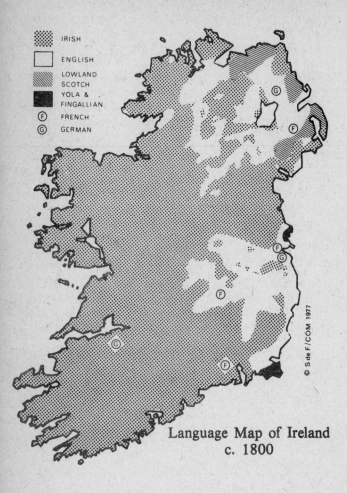

IRISH

ENGLISH

LOWLAND
SCOTCH

YOLA &
FINGALLIAN

Ⓕ FRENCH

Ⓖ GERMAN

© S de F /COM 1977

Language Map of Ireland
c. 1800

reinforced by Irish-speaking immigrants from Omeath in County Louth who established themselves in the Smithfield area.

In Dublin there were two Irish-speaking areas of long standing. One lay behind the north quays, bounded roughly on the west by Stoneybatter. A larger amount of Irish was to be found in the Liberties on the south side of the city, between Whitefriar Street and Thomas Street. Here, in Swift's Lane, a Baptist School was opened in 1815, where English was taught through the medium of Irish because it was found that the young pupils 'learn to read the language they have been accustomed to speak with greater facility than a foreign one'. Here, too, in Mitre Alley, in the shadow of St Patrick's Cathedral, one might see the Irish signboard of Michael O'Casey, a traditional physician, who plied the art of healing with the aid of numerous medical manuscripts written in Irish.

To summarise the linguistic situation about the year 1800, two provinces, Connacht and Munster, varied from being almost entirely to being mainly Irish-speaking; the situation was similar in north Leinster. In south Leinster, the counties of Dublin, Wicklow, Kildare, Carlow and south Wexford, were substantially English-speaking; Kilkenny and the remaining parts of Wexford were mainly Irish-speaking; and Laois and Offaly, were linguistically mixed. In Ulster, Irish was to be found in north-east Antrim, south Armagh, south Derry, north Tyrone and west Fermanagh. It was generally spoken in Cavan and Monaghan, and in County Donegal outside of the Lagan area in the east of the county and a few small English-speaking enclaves in other parts. Irish and English were to be found in most of the cities and towns, but English was the dominant language, the language of power, of social acceptance, of business and of trade.

This mixture was not exceptional by standards

elsewhere. If we want a comparable situation abroad, the territories of Bohemia and Slovakia, which constitute the modern state of Czechoslovakia, offer a remarkable similarity. There, in the year 1800 and for many years afterwards, much of the country spoke Slavic. There were also, however, extensive German-speaking areas. In the cities, German predominated overwhelmingly, and like English in Ireland, it was the language of officialdom, of business, of commerce and of the professions.

It is not easy to ascertain the numerical strength of the languages in Ireland around 1800. We may hazard that of the total population less than a third (or in round figures, about one and a half million people) spoke English only; some two million spoke Irish only; and another one and a half million were bilingual.

The first official census which provides linguistic statistics is that of 1851. The census is, however, unreliable in regard to language, a fact which the Census Commissioners rather diffidently acknowledge. According to that census the total Irish-speaking population was one and a half million, or 23% of the total population of the country. There are, however, some data in the components of that total which are hard to accept. For example, the Irish-speaking population of County Louth is given as 19,000 people, out of a total population of over 120,000. Only 51 persons in the county were returned as being unable to speak English. Yet in 1810, when John Gamble stayed with a shopkeeper friend of his in Drogheda, the largest and most important town in the county, he found that his acquaintance was obliged to employ a shopman at a large salary to conduct business for him in Irish. Gamble says of him, 'I suppose he can speak Irish very well, for he spoke English very badly.' In 1842 another visitor to the town, the German traveller, Kohl, described Drogheda as a very Irish town, and said that in it and in its neighbourhood there were very many

who could not speak English with ease or fluency.
About the same time the officials of the Ordnance
Survey were able to record the names of every street,
lane, alley and gate in Drogheda as they were known in
Irish. Yet according to the census figures of 1851 there
was only a handful of Irish speakers in Drogheda,
including a solitary monoglot speaker. Taking the
county at large, one Colonel Fortescue affirmed in
1823 that the proportion of the people who spoke Irish
was seven or eight to one. Since the Petty Sessions had
been established there some time previously, hardly a
day passed without the magistrates encountering
someone who could not speak English properly. A
German journalist, J. Venedy, who covered Daniel
O'Connell's Repeal campaign in 1843, found that the
landlady of the inn where he stayed in Dundalk knew
very little English, and he had a similar experience at
Castlebellingham, where this posed problems when
ordering breakfast. A Repeal meeting at Stabannon
was addressed in Irish by the Reverend Mr. King, a
Protestant minister, who directed his words especially
to those of his audience who did not know English.

None of this extensive life in Irish is revealed by the
census of 1851. Less than one-sixth of the total
population of the county were recorded as Irish
speakers, and of these, as has been said already, only
51 were returned as monoglots. It is hard to reconcile
these figures with the evidence of so many observers in
the years just before the Famine. Yet, if the data
provided by the census do not command great
credibility, they are significant in another way. They
may not show how far the people had travelled on the
road to anglicisation, but they pointed unmistakeably
in the direction they were going. It matters little
whether the statistics of this particular census were
correct or not; by the end of the century fact had
caught up with fiction, and a strange fact it was to be.

We can appreciate what was happening only by

distinguishing between the conventional language fluctuations of earlier times and the events of the later three-quarters of the nineteenth century. The earlier shifts in Ireland, which resulted in the assimilation to Irish or English speech of smaller language communities, were in accordance with natural processes of social development (or 'social mobilisation') which accompanies such things as literacy and literary activity, the growth of trade, better communications and greater mobility.

What was extensively happening by the middle of the nineteenth century cannot be explained in terms of social mobilisation alone. It developed largely independently of — even in the absence of — adequate factors of social mobilisation. It markedly demonstrates features of a social phenomenon which has been called 'collective behaviour' — that is, behaviour which is engaged in collectively by people and which is at variance with their traditional ways of doing things. It is characterised by panic, hysteria, or utopianism, or by any mixture of these emotions. This behaviour is particularly liable to occur in times of severe cultural strain. It represents an irrational hope of relieving the strain by trying to escape from the limitations of an intolerable reality. Essentially, collective behaviour seeks to short-circuit the constraints imposed by the nature of things. Among unsophisticated peoples we can see this behaviour for what it is, a reliance on magic. Thus in the last century the Sun Dance and the Ghost Dance Movements among American Indian tribes, and the current Cargo Cults among the natives of Melanasia, are examples of collective behaviour. These occur in communities whose whole way of life has been, or is being, undermined. In more sophisticated societies the need for action to relieve strain can also occur, but to meet the needs of more developed and more sophisticated mentalities, the action taken assumes culturally more

acceptable forms. At the present time, in a world beset
by unprecedented change, the cultural strains being
experienced by the young are enormous. It is not
surprising that this is also an age of proliferating cults,
sects, beliefs, and charismatic movements, all
promising utopia or the millenium, if only one follows
them.

Nineteenth-century Ireland underwent a similar
experience. The social opportunities and aspirations of
the post-Penal age became potentially attainable to a
people whose social and cultural institutions had been
so stunted that they were unable to cope with the
situation or even to offer a promise of readily providing
for newly-awakened needs. Not surprisingly, the
Ireland of the nineteenth century produced its crop of
utopian attitudes towards its problems. Here is one
example from a speech on Repeal by the Liberator
himself (who probably did not believe in his simplified
message, but knew that it would appeal to his
listeners): 'There is but *one* means for the complete
rescue of Ireland, and that is Repeal; but one thing on
which the welfare of all depends — Repeal. With
Repeal you will be happy, with Repeal you will become
rich, with Repeal you will obtain all you deserve and
strive for.'

It is not surprising that a similar approach should
have been adopted in the case of Ireland's linguistic
dilemma. Rather than spend time in making good the
centuries of neglect of the language, it seemed much
more sensible to short-circuit the task by adopting
English and thereby acquiring ready-made the
institutional aids to development available through that
language.

It is only by seeing it as a millenial or utopian
movement that the mass flight from the Irish language
becomes explicable. The methods used would not be
tolerated in any normal society under normal
conditions. The worst excesses were not imposed from

outside. The whole paraphernalia of tally sticks,
wooden gags, humiliation and mockery — often
enforced by encouraging children to spy on their
brothers and sisters, or on the children of neighbouring
townlands — were not the product of any law or official
regulation, but of a social self-generated movement of
collective behaviour among the people themselves.
Most of the reasons adduced for the suppression of the
Irish language are not so much reasons as
consequences of the decision to give up the language.
Thus, it is not just enough to say that the language
declined because it was excluded from the national
schools. For one thing, it was excluded from the
schools because the people in general had no interest in
ensuring a place for it there. They accepted the
ethnocentric Ascendancy viewpoint that Irish was a
backward language, and that even to speak it was a
positive hindrance to progress. Long before the
national schools became effective, the London
Hibernian Society, which had provided classes for
teaching Irish in its schools, reported a decline in the
classes because the parents were not in favour of them.
Far from wanting Irish in the national schools, the
parents and the teachers saw in the schools a means,
far beyond the requirements of any regulation, for
suppressing the language.

Apart from Archbishop MacHale very few men of
note protested against what happened. One of the few
who did was an official — Sir Patrick Keenan, then a
school inspector and later Commissioner of Education
in Ireland. In 1857 he castigated the failure of
managers and teachers in County Donegal to use the
Irish language as a teaching medium. The effect of this
fatuity, as he calls it in his official reports, was to
render the whole system of education a mere idle,
profitless waste of time. In describing what happened
in his native place in Tyrone, the poet John Montague
illustrates accurately what Keenan recounts more

prosaically, but equally vehemently, in his reports:

> Dumb,
> bloodied, the severed
> head now chokes to
> speak another tongue ...
>
> To slur and stumble
>
> in shame
> the altered syllables
> of your own name;
> to stray sadly home
>
> and find
> the turf-cured width
> of your parents' hearth
> growing slowly alien:
>
> In cabin
> and field, they still
> speak the old tongue.
> You may greet no one.

The parental attitude portrayed (accurately) in these lines is worth noting. It was an attitude not merely of favouring the acquisition of English, but of actively suppressing a knowledge of Irish, particularly among the young. This attitude was in evidence early in the century, but it became most pronounced in the decades immediately following the Great Famine. To some extent, this attitude helps to explain some of the surprising language statistics of the 1851 census. The Famine, however, marked a crucial point in the linguistic history of Ireland. It resulted in the death of about one million people, and in the immediate flight of another million. This meant a great numerical loss to Irish since it was among the sections of the population most affected by death and emigration that the language had been strongest.

The Famine had a further and more lasting effect. It left as legacy the fear of a recurrence. In order to escape this, to avoid being trapped, parents looked upon English as the key to the golden door of America, which they ought to give to their children. This produced an unusual linguistic phenomenon. The language shift began to occur more rapidly in the home than in the world outside. The census figures for 1861 demonstrate this. Of the population then between one and ten years of age less than 2% spoke Irish only. On the other hand, of those aged between 70 and 80 years, more than 4% spoke Irish only. Normally, one would expect to find that the home would prove more conservative than the market place, and that consequently there would be a greater proportion of young children than of old people who had not learned English, particularly when one considers that the old people in question had mixed with an English-regulated world for at least three score years and ten.

By the year 1900 the transformation was almost complete. The census of the following year showed that English had become the sole language of 85% of the population. Of the 15% who were Irish-speaking, a mere handful of 21,000 people, concentrated in the poorest and remotest parts of the country, were ignorant of English. By any standards this was a remarkable occurrence. Today, from the behavioural sciences, we know that such a dramatic cultural upheaval could not have taken place without the payment of some price. There is not space, nor is it within the terms of this paper, to consider here what that price might have been. Inevitably, a great deal was lost, resulting in a corresponding amount of social and cultural disorientation. As an old countryman, looking back on the changes which he had seen in the course of a long life, said to J. M. Synge in the year 1902, 'Now all this country is gone lonesome and bewildered and there's no man knows what ails it.'

Short Bibliography

Arthur, William. *The Life of Gideon Ouseley*. London, 1876

Charlotte Elizabeth (Mrs. Phelan). *The Works of Charlotte Elizabeth,* vol. I. New York, 1844

Gamble, John. *Sketches in Dublin and the north of Ireland*. London, 1811

Hume, Rev. Abraham. *Origins and Characteristics of the People of Down and Antrim*. Belfast, 1874

Hume, Rev. Abraham. *Remarks on the Irish Dialect of the English Language*. Liverpool, 1878

Kohl, J. G. *Travels in Ireland*. London, 1844

McQuige, James. *The Importance of Schools for Teaching the Native Irish Language*. London, 1818

Smelser, Neil J. *Theory of Collective Behaviour*. Routledge and Kegan Paul, London, 1967

Synge, J. M. *In Wicklow, West Kerry and Connemara*. Dublin, 1911

Twiss, Richard. *A Tour in Ireland in 1775*. Dublin, 1776 .

Venedy, J. *Ireland and the Irish during the Repeal Year, 1843*. Dublin, 1844

Warburton, J., and Whitelaw, J. *History of the City of Dublin,* vols. I and II. Dublin, 1818

The quotation is from John Montague's 'A Grafted Tongue', in *The Rough Field,* published by the Dolmen Press, Dublin, 1971.

DIALECT AND LITERATURE

BENEDICT KIELY

Dialect is a matter of idiom and intonation, just as language is, or the chatter of monkeys in the trees, or the carefully-balanced dialogues of rooks in a rookery, or the tumult of starlings in the coigns of an old building. Those who know the languages of rooks or monkeys may yet be able to distinguish localised usages. When a man in Bonniconlon pronounces the name Shligo it isn't the name as it would be pronounced by a man in Ballybough or Bunthorpe. Here in Dublin where I have spent most of my life I pass, believe it or not, for having an Ulster accent. Yet once in my own town in Tyrone a man told me that I had signs of what he, at that time, called a Free State accent. The ear as well as the tongue creates dialect, and although it is not usual to find that anyone who began life with Ulster vowel sounds will ever alter them or have them altered except by some major operation that has not yet been invented, yet, because of long residence among Free Staters, Munstermen, Leinstermen, Connachtmen, Kerrymen and the like, I found myself using idioms that immediately sounded unfamiliar, even faked, to my fellow Ulsterman.

By way of contrast I was once, in the State of Virginia, U.S.A., told that I had a southern accent, that is of the southern states of the U.S.A. And when I asked why that outrageous statement should be made I was asked to repeat the names of God and of Carolina. The explanation was simply that into the Carolinas, Virginia, Georgia, and so on, a lot of people with Ulster vowel sounds had once come, grabbing the land

and hunting the red men. The red men are as good as gone. Some of the Ulster vowel sounds remain. There's a county that I've heard of in Alabama where some of the people have, by and large, a Tyrone accent.

To say that dialects and variations within our language make for problems of communication is scarcely to announce any startling discovery. It is also easier for a German to speak to a Polynesian if the German speaks Polynesian or the Polynesian speaks German, or if the two of them speak Dutch or Hebrew. But in the simple act of talking, dialect presents itself naturally. When it comes to putting dialect down on the printed page the problems right away multiply. There is an ever-present danger of artificiality. There is the question of some sort of phonetic as against standard spelling. Then will the reader be able, without difficulty, to understand that spelling: and, further, if he does get to understand it, could he read it out aloud, and still make sounds in anyway resembling what the author had in his mind or ear-drums when he wrote the words down.

As in so many other things, including general history, for an understanding of Ireland take a look at Scotland. From the earliest relevant times, that is the time of the Scottish Chaucerians, Henryson, Dunbar and others, the relationship between the English used in Scotland and the language used by the mere English has been of vast interest.

Our own tentative grapplings with the angel of the English language began somewhere in the shadows of the seventeenth century, although it was not, as Seán de Fréine pointed out, until the nineteenth century that English really made the conquest to which the material triumph of the people who owned the language entitled it. This is neither to praise nor dispraise the nature of that triumph. But the Scots were more intensely engaged and for a much longer time, and the questions and answers relating to dialect were there much more clearly outlined. Burns is the most convenient example. The common assumption is that his genius revealed itself at its best when he was writing as he would have spoken to his father or to one of his rural beauties and not spelling out words as they were spelled out in the academies. The common assumption seems to be the truth, even if there is a lot to be said for the spenserian pieties of 'The Cottar's Saturday Night', and even as against 'The Jolly Beggars' and 'Tam O' Shanter'. Perhaps the whole divergence between standard and dialect may be measured by the distance between the cottar on his knees and Tam and the Beggars at their carousing: discipline, devotion and law in sharp contrast to nature and spontaneity. But in relation to this country, those byart leaves bestrowing the yird, or wavering like the bauchie bird: or that daimen icker in a thrave to which the wee sleekit, cowerin, timorous beastie was as much entitled to, as David was to the loaves of sacrifice — meant that Burns became a popular folk-author in Ulster, Catholic and Protestant, as he never was or could have been in any other part of Ireland. He still remained so in my boyhood: and I recall the local ragged rhymester saying to me, with a seriousness at which it was not possible to laugh, that: 'Burns was the best of us'. No other single poet that I can think of did as much for any other part of Ireland.

Yet even Burns, moving at his ease from the way they spoke on the farms to the way they wrote in the academies, and back again, does not fully point up the contrast between polite speech, as we may even yet call it, and dialect. But at about the same time John Wilson, an Edinburgh professor, wrote for Blackwood's magazine what today we would call a column, a series of journalistic entertainments under the title of 'Noctes Ambrosianae' and under the pen-name of Christopher North. The column took the shape of imaginary conversations in which the two chief participants were Wilson, or North, and James Hogg, the poet, known as the Ettrick shepherd, a sort of Patrick Kavanagh of his period who spent a lot of his time asleep on a sofa in Walter Scott's Abbotsford. It is interesting to see (in an amusing volume selected out of the column) the professor, or North, talking in the best standard English while the shepherd all the time delivers himself in the broadest of broad Scots. The shepherd has been laid low by the jaundice and North says: *'An obstructed condition of the duodenum, James.'* And the shepherd replies: 'You begin to hate and be sick o' things that used to be moist delightfu' [sic] as the sky, and streams, and hills, and the ee and voice and haun and breast o' woman. You dunner aboot the doors, dour an' dowie, and are seen settin' in nyeucks and corners, whare there's little licht, no mindin the cobwabs, or the spiders themselves droppin down among your unkempt hair. You canna say that you are unco ill either, but just a wee sickish — tongue furry, as if you had been lickin' a muff or a mawkin — and you observe, frae folk stanin wee back when you happen to speak to them — which is nae aften — that your breath's bad, though a week before it was as caller as clover.'

It is also interesting to note in the irony of things, that the author of most interest to the time we live in is not Scott, nor Professor Wilson, nor even Burns, but the much-laughed-at Ettrick Shepherd: and for a book in which there is not one word of dialect, a novel, *The Justified Sinner,* to abbreviate the title, which startlingly, and even better than Stevenson in Jekyll and Hyde illuminates the double mind of Scots calvinism and which has impressed such various writers as André Gide in France and the poet, Louis Simpson, in the U.S.A.

The homely speech of the Ettrick Shepherd is ordinary in idiom and construction, and only some of the words are odd. Yet my inability to present an exact reading of him as John Wilson would have had him speak, and as he probably did speak, simply underlines the way in which dialect in literature can create difficulties, not only to the tongue that is unfamiliar with it, but even to the eye. And the Scots experience is illuminating because it is exact and discernible. No modern Irish poet has so successfully struggled with two languages, standard and Lallans, as has the Scots poet Hugh Mac Diarmaid:

I amna fou sae muckle as tired — deid dune
It's gey and hard wark coupin' gless for gless
Wi' Cruivie and Gilsanquhar and the like,
And I'm no juist as bauld as aince I wes
The elback fankles in the coorse o' time,
The sheckle's no sae souple and the thrapple
Grows deef and dour: nae langer up and down
Gleg as a squirrel speils the Adam's apple.

All depending on what part of Ireland, or the neighbouring island, you come from the drunk man looking at the thistle takes a greater or lesser amount of getting used to. What gives it validity — and this is of general application — is that Mac Diarmaid does not write thus out of any rough, blunt desire for singularity, but because that, for him, is a natural mode of speech. And also, almost more than anything else Mac Diarmaid, the socialist, seems to fear a linguistic empire, to dread the hopelessness of being entangled in a language endangered by commercialism and the uniformity of what we call the media. For him dialect is a fortification for the poet, a guarantee of inexhaustible variety. The echoes of Scotland, of course, have crossed the narrow waters into this island, in dialect, spoken and written, as in other matters:

'Tis pretty to be in Baile Liosain
'Tis pretty to be in green Magh Luain,
But prettier to be in Newtownbreeda,
Beekin' under the eaves in June.

The cummers are out wi' their knittin' and spinnin'
The thrush sings frae the crib on the wa'
An' ower the white road, the clachan caddies
Play at their marlies an 'goalin' ba'.

That was Joseph Campbell, the mountainy singer,
getting the best out of words and phrases of Antrim
Scots: lesser poets, and prose-writers, have with
assiduity, sometimes painful to witness, and with
varying degrees of success, applied themselves to the
mixed speech of Ulster. The most effective of them was
by no means a major writer but a clerical scholar, a
doctor of divinity and a man who had devoted himself
to the study of the survival of older usages, even
Elizabethan usages, in the speech of rural Ulster: the
Rev. W. F. Marshall of Sixmilecross. It may come as a
surprise to many people to know that the lament of the
womanless mountainy farmer near Carrickmore in the
County Tyrone was the work of such a man: it has a
sure place in popular literature:

Wee Margit had no fortune
But two rosy cheeks wud plaze;
The farm of lan' was Bridget's,
But she tuk the pock disayse;
An' Margit she was very wee,
An' Bridget she was stout,
But her face was like a jail dure
With the bowlts pulled out.

So I swithered back an' forrit
Till Margit got a man,
A fella come from Mullaslin
An' left me just the wan.

I mind the day she went away,
I hid wan strucken hour,
An' cursed the wasp from Cullentra
That made me da so sour.

It may not be among the higher flights of lyric poetry, yet it is still immediately obvious that the reverend gentleman has observed his people and listened to them speaking: he had eyes and ears that any writer might be thankful for.

From survival from an older time and very obviously from the influence of Irish, even when that influence is hidden or unseen, our English derives and still retains a richness and colour that modern uniformity has not yet destroyed. Some of that richness may at times come between us and lucidity. We are a talkative and adjectival people, and the attitude of any reader towards such superfluity, and towards the exploitation of dialect, will be dictated by the nature of the ancient quarrel between classicism and romanticism, or between Hemingway and Fitzgerald, between whether literature is a matter of leaving out or putting in.

J. Braidwood in his very valuable study, *Ulster & Elizabethan English,* applauds the richness. He finds that the first and most striking parallel between Elizabethan English and Anglo-Irish is the sheer delight in language for its own sake. And the Elizabethan period was linguistically the most uninhibited in the history of the English language because it combined a maximum of art with a minimum of inhibition, and even the greatness of Shakespeare owed much to what Professor Wilcock has called his stimulating collaborator, the Elizabethan speaker and listener. This passage from Braidwood which I'll quote at some length, may be over-flattering to our national linguistic pride, that is: if you consider that richness, even recklessness, of vocabulary is a good thing. But it is a thoughtful and thought-provoking passage!

'The Elizabethans (or better the Tudors) discovered that the hitherto despised vernacular could be used with magnificent rhetorical effect, could even, because a living language of greater flexibility and inventiveness, surpass the traditional Latin. It was, however, during this Tudor period of unparalleled linguistic awareness that certain concepts began to evolve which industriously cultivated in the seventeenth and eighteenth centuries with their passion for standardisation and authority, made it virtually certain that we will never again reach the heights of Elizabethan speech and literature, for it was this age that first considerably formulated the notion of a Standard Literary English, of a standard of pronunciation, and of a standard spelling. Today probably only the Irishman, especially the southern Irishman, and some Welshmen, work in the Elizabethan linguistic, mastering the language, where the rest of us, with pusillanimous notions of correctness and good taste hammered into us at school, let the language master us. A child's progress along the highway of his native tongue — the byeways are prohibited — is impeded by deterrant notices at every step, and he spends far more time on analysis than synthesis, so that he can parse a sentence but not write one. We might occasionally remember that "the Elizabethans became eloquent before they became grammatical".

'If ever an age had the gift of the gab, that age was the Elizabethan. If ever a nation had the gift of the gab, that nation is the Irish. It is not suggested for a moment that the Irish inherited the gift from the Elizabethans, for the Irish gift is of ancient origin and the nation has long been notorious for loquacity.'

That passage is as close to the heart of the matter as makes no difference. But we should use it not merely to lay a flattering injunction to the soul but to examine the standardisation of speech and writing inevitable in our society: pressed on us by officialdom, by newspapers, radio and television (to talk of the media may be to use one of the worst of the clichés) and, perhaps, above all by the advertising industry. A standardisation that can affect our English and Irish and the variants thereof. Those young male singers with effeminate voices, coming from Belfast or Derry or where you will, and singing or trying to sing with the voices of Afro-Americans from Natchez, or Nashville or New Orleans may, and generally do, sound absurd. But it seems to me that they may be, if half unwittingly, in genuine search for a unique and meaningful idiom, for the phrase flavoured like a nut. It could, perhaps, be argued that they might be better off reading Shakespeare our loud to each other.

But in a world so tied up in a tight bundle, language must renew itself from such a variety of sources as was never before available: it must renew itself or die in clichés. But in the long run it is only an inborn taste, afterwards cultivated more by talkative company than by the rules of the academies, that will find the living phrase and record it in writing.

John Synge did, of course, make one of the best and certainly the most succinct statements on the matter and like Professor Braidwood he was, in his brief preface to 'The Playboy of the Western World', casting his mind back to the Elizabethans: 'In a good play, every speech should be as fully flavoured as a nut or apple, and, such speeches cannot be written by anyone who works among people who have shut their lips on poetry.'

The search for the unique phrase must always go along with the search for the theme that is unique and also universal, and Synge's preface to the *Playboy* pairs off in my mind with a celebrated passage from Marcus Antoninus: 'Whatever happens is as common and well-known as a rose in the spring or an apple in the autumn. Everywhere up and down, ages and histories, towns and families are full of the same stories.'

As deliberately as Wordsworth did, but with none of the unhappy accidents into which Wordsworth's solemnity betrayed him, Synge went searching for the living language of the people: and very deliberately in remote places where the words of the people had not (as he considered) been debased by schools and cities and newspapers.

'Among certain set apart in a most desolate stony place/Towards nightfall upon a race, passionate and simple like his heart.' The man, in the judgement of another poet, sought in the flavour and simplicity of that idiom the reflection of himself. He sought life also in the Gaelic idiom and movement that remained with people even in places where the language had died.

The ignorant absuridty, say, of the attack made on the language of Synge by St. John Ervine and others, who tried to argue that it was a mode of speech never heard on sea or land, was never so clearly brought home to me as one day on a road in Tyrone when I heard two countrymen talking in a language as rhythmical and stylised as Synge ever put on the stage: and that was not in the West nor South-West, nor in any Gaeltacht but in English-speaking country and among 'the preaching Luthers of the holy North'.

The advantages that dialect and local usage can bring to the writer is in giving a new sinew to his language, and a variety and a freshness: the disadvantages can at times be even more obvious in pedantry and eccentricity. The Irish novelists of the early nineteenth century found themselves in that way in a strange situation. They were caught between two languages, or, you might say, even somewhere in the centre between three: English, Anglo-Irish, and the Irish that was still plentiful on the tongues of the people. The occasional efforts made to render the Irish speech in an English phonetic spelling could at times be unhappy and they persisted right to the end of the century in the efforts made, say, by Jane Barlow to

catch in phonetics the speech of Irish people in the
villages that she called Lisconnel and Ballyhoy. She
was a woman in the clearest sympathy with the people
she wrote about, but she was the daughter of a vice-
provost of T.C.D., she herself had an academic turn of
mind and it was even listed in *Who's Who* that she
played the organ as her principal recreation. So with all
the pedantry of her disposition she set about to make
her Irish people talk real Irish. This could be the result.
An old lady called Moggy Goggin is complaining to
the lady who owns the animal about the behaviour of a
young brindled bull in a meadow called Long Leg.

'I thought I'd just tell you the way he's carrying on.
For when he come out first into the field he was
paiceable enough. But this last week or so it's
outrageous he's been. Time and again he's run at me;
and you know ma'am, I have to be crossin' the strame
and the corner of the Mount Field to get to the road
gate, and it's thereabouts he's keepin' continyal. Bedad,
I believe he has his eye on the house watchin' till I
come out. Yesterday he had me afeard to stir a step the
whole day, and I wantin' to get down to the town wid
me few eggs. They're sittin' in the basket yet. Young he
is, but he always was a passionate little crathur, and
more betoken, I distrust them brundly-coloured
bastes.'

And so on, in the best or worst style of Kitty the
Hare: which reminds me that I once saw one volume of
the plays of Synge that had belonged to Victor
O'Donovan Power the creator of Kitty the Hare. The
owner of the book had scrawled on the margins of the
pages quite ferocious comments on what he called the
Stage Irishness of Synge. It all depends, I suppose, on
one's point of view. For what Synge did was to
rationalise dialect and idiom with a melodic line, and to
enrich an orderly English by the use of dialect.
O'Casey did something similar for the speech of
Dublin and all through his autobiographical volumes

the rhythms and intonations of Dublin speech are clearly discernible. But there is nothing there to halt by pedantry or affectation any normal, intelligent reader of English.

From Maria Edgeworth onwards our writers of the nineteenth century were very conscious that they had a responsibility: they must delineate, as they called it, the Irish people for a readership that knew little about them and that quite often regarded them as ignorant and uncouth savages. Since William Carleton, Gerald Griffin and Michael and John Banim came closer than any others to the heart of the people they, meritably, saw that responsibility all the more seriously, and were the better able to line up to it.

Carleton was almost certainly a native speaker of Irish: his father and mother were, and his father was a story-teller, and his mother a renowned folk-singer. There was the famous story about her that when somebody asked her to sing an English version of *Bean an Fhir Ruaidh* she refused. She said that the English words and the music were like a man and his wife quarreling but that the Irish words melted into the music: like a man and his wife living in harmony. Her words, perhaps, could be taken as a permanent image of the quarrel, or the concorde, between standard English and the English spoken by people whose mouths, almost unknown to themselves, had been shaped by Irish.

Her son who became the first great Irish novelist made tremendous play with the vagaries of the speech of his countrymen, from the bog-Latin spoken by the voteen at Lough Derg, to the sesquipadalianism, or use of long words, of Mat Kavanagh, the hedge-schoolmaster, or of Denis O'Shaughnessy on that never-ending road to Maynooth. They were a people passionately interested in language, and only from such a people can the continual renewal of language ever come. The lips must never be closed on poetry.

THE ANGLO-IRISH IDIOM IN THE WORKS OF MAJOR IRISH WRITERS

JOHN GARVIN

The Anglo-Irish idiom is the mode of speech which is characteristic of the English language as spoken in Ireland. It owes its peculiarities to borrowings from the Irish language which took place mainly in the nineteenth century, when both Irish and English were in common use by a large proportion of the population. Douglas Hyde tells of his addressing a boy in the west of Ireland in Irish. The boy answered him in English. When a few sentences had been thus exchanged, Hyde asked the youth why he did not speak Irish in his replies. The boy said, 'Amn't I?', thereby revealing a domestic system of intercourse where the use of Irish was being artificially excluded from the younger generation in County Mayo in the late 1800s. A similar process had been in operation in the national schools since 1832. The result of this abnormally fast change in the medium of communication on the part of the majority of the Irish population was an equally-speedy evolution of the English idiom to adapt it to Irish ways of thinking and to the dialectical idiosyncrasies of the language which it was replacing. This evolution was an almost entirely subconscious adjustment of their mode of speech by the ordinary, illiterate or poorly-educated population intent on maintaining forms of self-expression appropriate to their naturally lively intelligence. The first effects of the evolution were the mispronunciation and misuse of English words and phrases which came to be classified as the Irish brogue, Irish bulls and various other forms of verbal blunders and were ascribed to Irish ignorance and intellectual retardedness. Another effect which was more slowly recognised was the enrichment of the English language tnat had been effected by its being crossed (so to speak) with the Irish. There was little conscious recognition of this until Douglas Hyde initiated the campaign for the revival of Irish and published his editions of religious songs, love songs and folk tales, taken down from Irish speakers, and of stories from Gaelic manuscripts. These were accompanied by English translations which often gave literal English renderings of the Irish originals. The intelligent reader was quick to realise the similarity between these versions of traditional and literary Irish and the idiomatic forms of English which the ordinary people had evolved for themselves when confronted with the task of doing their thinking and talking in an alien tongue.

It was only a matter of time before Irish writers became aware of the potential of the new medium for literary expression. Once this potential was recognised, the history of Anglo-Irish literature became the efforts of successive writers to use the medium artistically, with varying degrees of respect for its idiomatic integrity.

The language of Lady Gregory's plays was, she says, based on the speech of the people in the barony of Kiltartan surrounding her home at Coole, Co. Galway. The literary dialect which she based on this speech was called 'Kiltartan' or 'Kiltartanese'. It was undoubtedly based on the local speech, but Lady Gregory too frequently assumed that all the people spoke Kiltartanese always, even in the heroic past and in the days of old romance. Yeats, in a note to *Red Hanrahan,* thanked Lady Gregory 'who helped me to rewrite the stories in the beautiful country speech of Kiltartan'. One of the stories in the section of the *Red Hanrahan* volume called *The Secret Rose,* 'Of Costello

the Proud, of Oona the daughter of Dermott, and of
the Bitter Tongue', is in fact a reduction of the beautiful
seventeenth-century love story of Una Bhán and
Tomás Láidir Costello into bad Kiltartanese. The
historical setting is mistaken, the local scenes are
misplaced and the version of the ghostly element in the
story suggests the early influence on Yeats of Madame
Blavatsky. Yet in his poem, also called *The Secret
Rose,* Yeats used the Una Bhán legend to brilliant
effect, a Gaelic description of her lustrous hair being
the original of his lines:

*A woman of so shining loveliness
That men threshed corn at midnight by a tress
A little stolen tress.*

Yeats truly said:

*I have no speech but symbol, the pagan speech I made
Amid the dreams of youth.*

It was in this 'pagan speech' and not in the Anglo-
Irish idiom that he created his 'Celtic Twilight',
between the shadow of Ben Bulben and the shadow of
the Pre-Raphaelite dream.

Austin Clarke, on the other hand, a poet who knew
the original language and authentic background of the
traditional Gaelic tales, could re-tell them in well-knit
Anglo-Irish verse incorporating the assonance of older
poetry, as in the following lines from *The Vengeance of
Finn*:

*Flower-quiet in the rush-strewn sheiling
At the dawntime Grainne lay,
While beneath the birch-topped roof the sunlight
Groped upon its way
And stooped over her sleeping white body
With a wasp-yellow ray.*

The next generation of writers, including Liam O'Flaherty, Seán Ó Faoláin and Frank O'Connor, seem to have discounted the value of the idiom. They used it, but only perfunctorily, and they did little to develop it artistically. They may, perhaps, have thought that it had outlived its artistic validity. In any event, I now propose to concentrate on the use of the idiom by those writers in whose works it was consciously used as an integral part of their art and developed or overdeveloped and, perhaps, in that process, developed out of existence.

Whether the literary output of Somerville and Ross is or is not part of the canon of major Anglo-Irish writing, they deserve mention at this point as being the first consciously to use the Anglo-Irish idiom artistically and as a means of seriously delineating Irish national character and a way of thinking which was different from the English way of thinking. Before them Irish popular speech in literature was simply the brogue represented by misspelt words intended to reproduce the mispronunciation of standard English by derisory specimens of a lesser breed. In their *Children of the Captivity* Somerville and Ross write:

> The vitalising power is in the rhythm of the sentence, the turn of phrase, the knowledge of idiom and of, beyond all, the attitude of mind ... Want of perception of word and phrase and turn of thought means more than mere artistic failure, it means want of knowledge of the wayward and shrewd and sensitive minds that are at the back of the dialect. The very wind that blows softly over brown acres of bog carries perfumes and sounds that England does not know; the women digging the potato land are talking of things that England does not understand. The question that remains is whether England will ever understand.

(Echoes of these scenes and sounds that England did
not understand were later versified by another hand
and sung around the world under the title of 'Galway
Bay'.)

Here is how Somerville and Ross give Slipper's
account of the steeplechase in which Driscoll was
riding a mare, which Slipper had just given 'a couple o'
dhraws o' th' ash plant across the butt o' the tail, the
way I wouldn't blind her':

> '. . . before you could say "Shnipes", she was
> standin' on her two ears beyant in th' other field.
> I declare to ye, on the vartue of me oath, she
> stood that way till she reconnoithered what side
> Driscoll would fall, and she turned about then
> and rolled on him as cosy as if he was meadow
> grass.' Slipper stopped short; the people in the
> doorway groaned appreciatively; Mary Kate
> murmured 'The Lord save us' — 'The blood was
> druv out through his nose and ears', continued
> Slipper, with a voice that indicated the cream of
> the narration, 'and you'd hear his bones crackin'
> on the ground' . . . 'Was he hurt, Slipper?' asked
> Flurry (Knox) . . .'

While Somerville and Ross were about the first to
lay down the principles governing the artistic use of
idiom, John Synge came to much the same conclusions
from studying the vocabulary and turns of speech that
he heard used by beggar-women and ballad singers in
and around Dublin and by the sheepfarmers of County
Wicklow and the cottiers of Mayo. He also had a
knowledge of the Gaelic vernacular picked up chiefly
in the Aran Islands.

In *The Playboy of the Western World* these demotic
vernaculars are interfused. In his preface to the play he
postulated the artistic use of 'a popular imagination
that is fiery and magnificent and tender'.

'I stood a while outside wondering would I have a right to pass on or to walk in and see you.' Here the phrase 'have a right' is used to mean 'should'. The word is a translation of the Irish *cóir* and is used in the sense of the proper or permissible thing to do. Shortly afterwards, in the dialogue between Shaun and Pegeen Mike, Shaun uses a synonym for the word 'right' in its strict English usage: 'You'll have no call to complain.' The word 'call' here is the Irish *cáll,* meaning 'cause' or 'claim', and it was in common use in Ireland (including Dublin) forty years ago.

'If you're a dunce *itself,* you've a right to know.' Here, the word *itself* is an Irishism, the sense being, 'Even if you are a dunce, you should know.'

The words to which I have drawn attention are examples of the authentic Anglo-Irish idiom, but when Christy Mahon is cross-examined as to the nature of his mysterious crime, there is more emphasis on what Somerville and Ross called 'the rhythm of the sentence':

> 'Were you off east, young fellow, fighting bloody wars for Kruger and the freedom of the Boers?'

Synge is by no means loath to participate in the Irish predilection for picturesque recitative but it is a question whether he is drawing on his Anglo-Irish idiom or whether that idiom has suffered a seachange in the tides of his own poetic imagination. Christy's father is ordering him to wed the Widow Casey, 'a walking terror from beyond the hills, and she two score and five years ... with a limping leg on her and a blinded eye, and she a woman of noted misbehaviour with the old and young'.

> 'Go on,' says he, 'or I'll have the divil making garters of your limbs tonight' ... With that the sun came out between the cloud and the hill, and

it shining green in my face. 'God have mercy on your soul,' says he, lifting a scythe. 'Or on your own,' says I, raising the loy. . . . He gave a drive with the scythe, and I gave a lep to the east. Then I turned round with my back to the north and I hit a blow on the ridge of his skull, laid him stretched out, and he split to the knob of his gullet. [Here, 'laid him stretched out' is a relative clause with the relative 'that' omitted.]

Pegeen Mike is eager to have Christy as potboy in the pub: 'If I had that lad in the house I wouldn't be fearing the looséd kharki cut-throats or the walking dead.' Here Synge has an accent over the 'e' in 'loosed', so that the actress is required to pronounce it 'looséd': this archaic poeticising of the vernacular lends an air of unreality to the dialogue: naturalism gives way to melodramatic phantasy.

Christy's description of his father has a marvellous simile based on Synge's own knowledge, as a naturalist, that the ashtree is the last of the larger trees to leaf in Spring:

'. . . if you seen him and he after drinking for weeks, rising up in the red dawn, or before it maybe, and going out into the yard as naked as an ashtree in the moon of May, and shying clods against the visage of the stars till he'd put the fear of death into the banbhs and the screeching sows.'

There is a growing implication that Christy is a natural poet, intended perhaps to justify Synge's increasing commitment to poetic language:

I was lonesome all times, and born lonesome, I'm thinking, like the moon of dawn.

Christy's father, when he has been persuaded that

he is mad in claiming Christy to be his son, exclaims:

> Oh, I'm raving with a madness that would fright
> the world! ... There was one time I seen ten
> scarlet divils letting on they'd cork my spirit in a
> gallon can; and one time I seen rats as big as
> badgers sucking the lifeblood from the butt of
> my lug; but I never till this day confused that
> dribbling idiot with a likely man. I'm destroyed
> surely ... and I a terrible and fearful case, the
> way that there I was one time, screeching in a
> straightened waistcoat, with seven doctors
> writing out my sayings in a printed book.

James Stephens' use of the Anglo-Irish idiom is
more homely and restrained; it is also a discipline
which limits the verbose philosophising to which he is
otherwise addicted.

> A Leprecaun from Gort na Cloca More was here
> today. They'll *give it to you* for robbing their pot
> of gold. [This means that they will punish him.]

Of Caitilin, the missing daughter of Meehawl Mac
Murracha, there is this pessimistic premonition which
is a little suggestive of Synge:

> Maybe the girl was lying dead in the butt of a
> ditch with her eyes wide open, and she staring
> broadly at the moon in the night and the sun in
> the day until the crows would be finding her out.

But Stephens has an individualistic talent both
peculiar to himself and also owing something to the
urban idiom of demotic Dublinese:

> 'Did you ever hear,' said Meehawl, 'of the man
> that had the scalp of his head blown off by a gun,

and they soldered the bottom of the tin dish to the top of his skull the way you could hear his brains ticking inside of it for all the world like a Waterbury watch?'

In that sentence the phrase 'the way' is Anglo-Irish for 'so that' or 'with the result that'. Later, we find: 'Be sure and hold him tight the way we can have a good look at him.'

To the little girl's talk of going to bed, the Leprecaun replies, 'Why wouldn't you?' — meaning, 'of course'.

Then we have the pathetic but somewhat repetitious lamentations of the old woman, concluding:

'Ah, God be with me! I wish there weren't stones in my boots, so I do, and I wish to God I had a cup of tea and a fresh egg. Ah, glory be, my old legs are getting tireder every day, so they are. Wisha, one time — when himself was in it — I could go about the house all day long, cleaning the place, and feeding the pigs and the hens and all, and then dance half the night, so I could: and himself proud of me ...'

As in Synge, we find Stephens using the words 'right' and 'call' in the senses already described: 'You have a right to be ashamed of yourselves'; 'What call would men like us have to go mixing and meddling with their [i.e. the gods'] high affairs?'

In the last fifty years, the increased mobility of the Irish population had reciprocal influences on the rural and the Dublin idioms. The migrants to Dublin brought the idioms of the provincial towns and rural areas to the city and the Dublin idiom came more readily and widely into use in the country.

Seán O'Casey uses a blend of both — a Dublin vocabulary used in the phraseology that is more widely characteristic of the Anglo-Irish idiom: I give some examples from *Juno and the Paycock*:

'I'll run round to Ryan's — I know it's a great house o'
    Joxer's' (I know it is a pub which Joxer usually likes
    to frequent);

'A Mickey Dazzler' — Dublinese of the 1920s for 'a
    masher', 'a ladykiller';

'chiselurs' — youngsters;

'the kisser' — the mouth;

'You could sing that if you had an air to it' (that is
    clearly true).

O'Casey writes a number of words ending in 'd' with
the 'd' silent:

'hole' (hold), 'poun' (pound), 'hans' (hands).

In *'The Plough and the Stars'* we find:

'There's kissin' and cuddlin' in it', i.e. some forms of
kissing and cuddling are more improper than others.
To accord with the exact idiom O'Casey should have
repeated the words, as Joyce does when he has 'Skin-
the-Goat' say, 'there are wrecks and wrecks',
suggesting that a particular wreck in Galway Bay was
different from other wrecks in that it was engineered in
order to block a harbour development scheme.

'What's the foostherin' for now?' Here we have an
English verbal form of the Irish noun, fustar, fuss. We
find the same form in Joyce's *Ulysses,* but it is
misprinted 'fostering' (in *The Lotus Eaters*).

There is a gem of Anglo-Irish repartee in the
argument between The Covey and Fluther about the
origin of life:

Fluther: Mollycewels! What about Adam an' Eve?
The Covey: Well, what about them?
Fluther: What about them, *you*?

The second person vocative is here used to insist that
the point is one which the person addressed, not the
speaker, should consider.

Another complex Anglo-Irish turn of speech is in
'Houl on there, Rosie!'

'What are you houldin' on out of you for?'

That is, why are you speaking to restrain me from getting treated to a drink? ('out of you' is borrowed from the Irish to signify something said).

I now come to Joyce. The Anglo-Irish idiom in *Ulysses* is reserved particularly for the vernacular of those characters who specialise in satire, censure, political controversy and comedy. Poetry, philosophy, dramatic criticism and rhetoric are rendered in other styles. Joyce takes some freedom with the idiom when it suits him but he can be exact when he wishes as in the milkwoman's reckoning of her bill: 'Well, it's seven mornings a pint at twopence is seven twos is a shilling and twopence over and these three mornings a quart at fourpence is three quarts is a shilling and one and two is two and two, sir.'

Bloom's meditations are generally presented in an urban, neutral style, but there is the occasional Irishism, as in *Lotus Eaters,* 'Up with her on the car', a rendering in English of the Irish *suas léithi,* signifying motion. Or, on the subject of articles which people leave behind them in trains and cloak rooms, 'What do they be thinking about?' Here, Bloom uses the English version of the Irish habitual form of the verb 'to be'.

The unintroduced first person singular narrator in *The Cyclops* reserves the cream of his satire for Bloom: 'that can be explained by Science, says Bloom. It's only a natural phenomenon ... Phenomenon! The fat heap he married is a nice old phenomenon with a back on her like a ballalley.' Eventually, however, he admits that even Bloom has his points: 'I declare to my antimacassar if you took up a straw from the bloody floor and if you said to Bloom: *Look at, Bloom, do you see that straw? That's a straw.* Declare to my aunt he'd talk about it for an hour so he would and talk steady.'

Davy Byrne, the Duke Street publican is asked for a tip for the winner of the Gold Cup: 'I wouldn't do anything at all in that line, Davy Byrne said. It ruined many a man the same horses.' This sentence, undivided by any comma to indicate that the substantive comes at the end, would be closer to the Irish idiom from which it derives if it were phrased: It's many a man they ruined the same horses.

A non-English student of English and Anglo-Irish is probably in the best position to make an objective and systematised analysis of the deviations of our idiom from the English norm. In a Netherlands periodical, *English Studies,* 24, 1942, G. J. Visser, writing on 'James Joyce's *Ulysses* and Anglo-Irish', outlined the forms of speech found in *Ulysses* which are not current outside Ireland (except perhaps under Irish influence). These are:

1. The word *and* performing the function of a pronominal relative clause, e.g., out with him *and* little Alf holding on to his elbow *and* he shouting like a stuck pig. (Here Visser might have pointed out that 'out with him' is also an Irishism.)
2. Omission of the relative pronoun, e.g., who is this was telling me?
3. Past (perfect) tense expressed by use of *after*: 'sure I'm after seeing him not five minutes ago' (this is Alf Bergan on Paddy Dignam who, in fact, had been buried in Glasnevin that morning).
4. *I do be* used as a habitual present: 'like the droughty clerics do be fainting for a pussful' (this, however, was intended by Joyce as a parody of Synge: I have already quoted a genuine use of this form by Bloom: 'What do they be thinking about?').
5. Unintroduced dependent questions: 'I just called to ask is she over it?'
6. The use of *on* as a dative of disadvantage, e.g., 'You won't play the saint *on* me any more.' A clearer example would be Bloom's meditation on Martin Cunningham's 'awful drunkard of a wife. Setting up house for her time after time and then pawning the

furniture on him every Saturday.' Or, better still, not from Joyce but from Irish annals, the dread rite of excommunication: 'they were quenching the candles on him'.

Other Irishisms in *Ulysses* noted by Visser are:

'You can cod him up to the *two* eyes.'

'My *two* hands.'

'My wife has *the* typhoid.'

'Spiffing *out of him* in Irish.'

Finnegans Wake abounds in Anglo-Irish idiom — it is indeed the basic dialect of the book — but it is subsumed into the stirabout of 'slanguage' which leaves the book adrift in a polyglottic sea of verbomania. I have, however, selected a passage which will be recognised to contain the rhythm and raciness characteristic of the Anglo-Irish idiom, whatever about its literal intelligibility. There are two overlying themes in it — the woods of Foclut near the Western shore, from which St. Patrick heard the voices of people begging him to come back to Ireland and, as the National Apostle, walk once more amongst them. The other is Parnell's appeal to his Parliamentary Party that they should not throw him to the wolves. Here the Woods of Foclut become the Wolves of Foclut. The underlying suggestion is that if Joyce himself, 'the National Apostate' were to return to Ireland he would be thrown to the wolves.

'— The woods of fogloot! O mis padredges!

'— Whisht awhile, greyleg! The duck is rising and you'll wake that stand of plover. I know that place better than anyone. Sure I used to be always over there at my grandmother's place, Tear-nan-Ogre, my little grey home in the west, in or about Mayo when the long dog gave tongue and they coursing the marches and they straining at the leash. — Follow me up Tucurlugh! That's the place for the claine oysters, Polldoody, County Conway — Do you know my cousin, Mr. Jasper Dougal that keeps the Anchor on the mountain, the parson's son, Jasper of the Guns, Pat Whateveryournameis?

'— Dood and I dood. The wolves of Fochlut! By Whydoyoucallme? Do not flingamejig to the twolves!

'— Turcafiera and that's a good wan right enough! Wooluvs no less!'

Joyce's original material was always simple: it was his treatment of it, his multiplication of meanings by puns, neologisms, telescopic words, borrowings from foreign languages, that makes his text complex.

Scribbledhobble, a notebook of phrases compiled by him in 1923 for use in *Finnegans Wake,* contain simple phrases probably culled from his wife's conversations. Here are some of them:

'Made much of him'; 'I was (i.e. I went) to see her'; 'will I do as I am?' (i.e. may I go out dressed as I am?); 'he looked at the time'; 'he couldn't lay his hands on it'; 'back he went'; 'a knock came to the door'; 'can't believe a word out of his mouth'; 'I heard from home' (i.e. I got a letter from my parents' house); 'is that any place to put (your dirty shoes)?'

In conclusion I give the last words of Anna Livia Plurabelle (the waters of the Liffey flowing to meet their father the sea): this is the end of *Finnegans Wake,* and will illustrate the idiom, the music and the rhythm of that enigmatic volume:

> Loonely in me loneness. For all their faults. I am passing out. O bitter ending! I'll slip away before they're up. They'll never see. Nor know. Nor miss me. And it's old and old it's sad and old it's sad and weary I go back to you, my cold father, my cold mad father, my cold and feary father, till the near sight of the mere size of him, the moyles and moyles of it, moananoaning makes me seasilt saltsick and I rush, my only, into your arms. I see them rising! Save me from those terrible prongs! Two more. Onetwo moremens more. So.

Avelaval. My leaves have drifted from me. All.
But one clings still. I'll bear it on me. To remind
me of Lff! So soft this morning ours. Yes. Carry
me along, taddy, like you done through the toy
fair. If I seen him bearing down on me now under
whitespread wings like he'd come from
Arkangels, I sink I'd die down over his feet,
humbly dumbly, only to washup. Yes, tid.
There's where. First. We pass through grass
behush the bush to. Whish! A gull. Gulls. Far
calls. Coming, far! End here. Us then. Finn,
again! Take. Bussoftlhee, mememormee! Till
thousendthee. Lps. The keys to. Given! A way a
lone a last a loved a long the

THE COLLECTORS OF
IRISH DIALECT MATERIAL

E. G. QUIN

When the collector of dialect material refers to 'The English Language in Ireland' he means, in more precise terms, the English language as spoken in Ireland, the ordinary language of everyday verbal intercourse, in other words the vernacular. And unfortunately interest in vernacular is a modern thing, at any rate at a scholarly level, so that our main source of information regarding ordinary speech in past centuries is usually the play or the novel, where vernacular is used mainly for comic effect and is open to the charge of inaccuracy and certainly to that of incompleteness. This means that when one comes to speak of collectors of Anglo-Irish material there is very little to be found before the latter half of the nineteenth century.

I begin with Charles Vallancey, who was born at Windsor in 1721 and died at the ripe old age of 91 in 1812. By profession he was a military engineer, and in 1762 he became engineer in ordinary in Ireland. He was promoted to Lt.-General in 1798, and to general in 1803, the year in which he reached the age of 82. Among his engineering activities may be mentioned the plans for one of those pretty bridges over the Liffey, the Queen's Bridge, since renamed Mellows Bridge, and a general plan for the defence of Dublin.

However, it is as a scholar and antiquarian that he is remembered, and his activities in this direction brought him membership of the Royal Irish Academy and fellowship of the Royal Society.

The edifice of modern scholarship is built on the detritus of the scholarship of previous generations, and it is sobering to imagine what will be thought of our own efforts in this direction in 150 to 200 years' time. Yet even this kind of allowance hardly accounts for the wildness of Vallancey's books and theories. For, as his biographer says, in his *Collectanea de rebus hibernicis* and other works, his facts are never trustworthy and his theories are invariably extravagant. One of his favourite pursuits was what he called 'collating' Irish, or Iberno-Celtic as he called it, with a wide variety of other languages, from those of Africa to the Algonquin languages of North America. Admittedly, the science of comparative philology, the assigning of languages to different families, has to proceed to a large extent by trial and error, and the first results are based on purely superficial resemblances. Indeed, it is only in the last 150 years or so that really rigorous methods have been evolved. In the eighteenth century the field was still wide open, and who is to blame Vallancey for exploring the possibilities of the linguistic affinities of Irish? What is less easy to forgive him is the fact that the Irish material he offered in his *Essay on the Celtic languages,* which he published in 1781, was frequently inaccurate and misinterpreted and indeed sometimes, apparently, quite imaginary. The fact is that he was that most awkward kind of person, a man of great learning and very little judgment. And even his learning is in question, for although he produced a grammar of the Irish language (in 1782) its confused and inaccurate arrangement shows that he can hardly have really acquired the vernacular or read genuine texts.

All of this must leave us with reservations about Vallancey's contribution to Anglo-Irish studies. However, for better or for worse he read a paper to the Royal Irish Academy in 1788 on the 'Language, Manners, and Customs of an Anglo-Saxon Colony settled in the Baronies of Forth and Bargy, in the County of Wexford, in 1167, 1168, and 1169'. And to this he appended a short list of words in his view peculiar to the district. The account of the manners and customs of the people of the district is sober and straightforward if a little idealistic, and the 300 or so local words he lists have all the appearance of genuineness. This is in such sharp contrast with the extravagance of his other works that one suspects the presence of another hand, and in fact it has been claimed that he 'lifted' this material from the next collector I have to mention. At all events it is extremely unlikely that he went to Wexford and recorded the words himself orally. The important thing is, however, that they are there, that he is the first in the published field. His mode of transcription, of course, gives us very little clear idea of how the words were pronounced. What, for instance, are we to make of *aloghe* 'below', *arich* 'the morning', *ligt* 'light', *riaught* 'right' or *zichel* 'such'?

From the vagaries of Vallancey we turn with some relief to the sober, factual work of Jacob Poole. Poole was a Quaker landowner in County Wexford, and as he died in 1827 was more or less a contemporary of Vallancey's. Like Vallancey, he had linguistic and antiquarian interests, at any rate where Wexford was concerned, but unlike Vallancey did not get round to publishing the results of his investigations. His glossary of words from Forth and Bargy was not published till after his death, when William Barnes printed it, in 1867. It runs to some 1200 or 1300 items, and very frequently the editor has inserted some explanatory notes, more particularly about parallels from English dialects in England. Thus under *fash* 'confusion, shame' he has added the note '*fash,* Northern England, to tire, tease, trouble'. This is of course French *fâcher,* and the term is known mainly from Scots English. It is interesting to find it in Wexford.

We come now to a more general and more modern work, that of P. W. Joyce, who at the beginning of this century produced a number of works dealing with Irish life and culture: *A Social History of Ancient Ireland, A Child's History of Ireland, The Origin and History of Irish Names of Places, Old Celtic Romances, A Grammar of the Irish Language, Irish Music and Song, Old Irish Folk Music and Song,* and in 1910 the most important for us, *English as we Speak it in Ireland.*

I do not know to what extent these books are nowadays read, but they have probably done quite a bit to introduce people to Irish culture. In them Joyce addressed himself to school classes and the general reader rather than to serious scholars, and this has tended to detract somewhat from his reputation among the latter. This is a pity, for there is much of value in his work, and his *English as we Speak it in Ireland* contains a good deal of information not available elsewhere. And though he rather puts one off by stating in his preface that 'this is essentially a subject for popular treatment', a statement which has been shown by these essays to be not altogether true, one cannot afford to neglect his book.

Joyce tells us that the work is the result of twenty years' collecting, albeit desultory collecting, that he drew on his own memory, on answers to a letter in the Irish newspapers in 1892 (he lists over 150 persons from whom he received information in one way or another), on the works of Irish writers of novels, on works on the subject already in print, and his own notes.

This is essentially the method (except for the memory work) used in the work I shall deal with next, Wright's *English Dialect Dictionary* (to which Joyce himself was a contributor). The difference between the two lies in the difference in objective, Wright's work being directed to the scholar, Joyce's to the layman who seeks merely general instruction and amusement. Of the latter Joyce gives plenty, especially in his chapters entitled 'Exaggeration, Redundance', 'Comparisons' and 'A Variety of Phrases'. On the other hand chapters like 'Sources of Anglo-Irish Dialect' and 'Grammar and Pronunciation' are more serious in tone, the latter in fact not a bad summary at all of the more obvious features of Anglo-Irish speech; it is particularly attractive when he gives quotations from the English poets to show how English some Irish pronunciations in fact are or were, as in Cowper's

> God moves in a mysterious way
>   His wonders to perform
> He plants His footsteps in the sea
>   And rides upon the storm

which needs no comment. Or in Pope's

> Dreaded by fools, by flatterers besieged
> And so obliging that he ne'er obliged

with a pronunciation of *oblige* usual, according to Joyce, with all classes in County Kildare, at any rate in 1910.

It would obviously be unfair to apply the methods of rigorous criticism to a book of this kind. But the serious scholar must regret that such a wealth of information as it contains could not have been accompanied by more exact references to sources.

Though all these works have their value, their authors hardly come into the category of great collector, for by this title must surely be meant a man who has devoted a lifetime or a very big portion of a lifetime to a large work, a *magnum opus*. And so it is time to say something about the important *English Dialect Dictionary,* by the Yorkshireman Joseph Wright. Its claim on our attention here is that Wright drew extensively on Irish sources. And even if he had not his work would always have to be consulted in order to place our own kind of English in perspective. I hope to give an example of what I mean by this at a later stage.

Joseph Wright was born in 1855 and died in 1930. His father had died young, and Joseph had to work hard in a Bradford mill to help to keep the family going. He received little or no formal education. In fact, he educated himself. This he did very efficiently, for in his teens, having first taught himself to read and write English, he was hard at work, after the day's labours in the mill, learning French and German.

In 1876, having saved £40, he managed a visit to Heidelberg. In 1882 he was off again to Germany, this time for six years. For the purposes of his future career he could not have arrived at a better time. His interest in linguistics was steadily increasing, particularly in the area of comparative philology. In Germany Wright was in his natural element, and to the end of his long life he remained a philologist in the German tradition.

In 1888 he was appointed to a small lecturing post in Oxford. By now he was competent in all the Germanic languages, especially in their older forms, and taught them extensively. In 1890 he became deputy professor of comparative philology at Oxford, and though his appointment to full professor did not take place till 1901 his standing and reputation were now steadily increasing (he was later, in 1906, to receive an honorary doctorate from Dublin University). And with his wide knowledge of phonetics and philology he was the obvious choice as editor when the general idea of an English dialect dictionary began to take root.

The work we now know as the *Oxford Dictionary* was first projected by the London Philological Society in 1858. It was realised at an early stage that there were large numbers of words, which, though English, were not in general use and could not be regarded as standard. It would be a pity, however, if these were not recorded in some way, and in order to preserve them the English Dialect Society was founded in 1873 and collection of material began with a dialect dictionary as the ultimate object. It attracted members from all over what were then the British Isles. These all made collections of dialect words and sent them in, and by the time the Society was wound up in 1896 it had been the means of publishing eighty volumes on particular English dialects.

In 1887 a formal proposal was made to Wright that he should undertake the editorship of a dialect dictionary. By 1890 the project was under way. The material already collected by the English Dialect Society was handed over to Wright. It consisted of some million slips weighing about one ton. Perhaps I should explain that in indexing or in compiling a dictionary all the items have to be written out on individual pieces of paper, usually called slips, and these then put into alphabetical order. A million slips must have been a daunting sight, yet even this amount Wright deemed insufficient for adequate documentation. He forthwith began a campaign to obtain helpers, and soon had a miniature army of about 600 correspondents. These went through books, newspapers and so on for dialect words, and sent him their collections at his headquarters, called 'the workshop', at Oxford.

But apart from the formidable intellectual and indeed physical task of compiling the dictionary itself there was another obstacle to be overcome. Money for printing was needed. And surprising as it may seem, Wright was quite unable to induce English publishing firms to undertake the work and face the financial risk involved. As he was to write later, 'it was conclusively proved that no publisher would undertake the work; and the sole method that remained was for the editor to publish it by subscription at his own pecuniary risk'.

Then began the campaign to obtain patrons and subscribers. These latter were to pay a pound a year and receive in return two parts per annum. Wright was soon able to publish an initial list of patrons, among them Edward Dowden, professor of English in Dublin University. The immediate object was to obtain 1000 subscribers, in other words £1000, before beginning on the actual work. In fact by June 1895 he had 750 and felt justified in making a start and preparing material for the press. The workshop then went into action. Wright had one senior assistant and two unskilled juniors. Later there were some increases, but the actual staff at Oxford was never very large. The real strength of the project lay in the hundreds of readers and contributors scattered over the British Isles, among them a fair number from Ireland. From all of these there came in a continuous stream of material which was incorporated with what was already there as the work progressed.

In the meantime Wright applied for a Civil List pension, and had a memorial drawn up and sent to Arthur Balfour, First Lord of the Treasury. Among the distinguished signatories to this document was Robert Atkinson, professor of Sanskrit in Dublin University, who wrote: 'It does seem strange that while money is flung away recklessly on all sorts of absurdities, there should be found no wealthy merchant who would honour himself by placing at your disposal the requisite funds for the suitable completion of . . . this admirably executed work.' In 1896 a grant of £600 from the Royal Bounty was given in aid of the publication of the dictionary. This was to cover three years, and in 1898 the news came through of a Civil List pension of £200 per annum.

Meanwhile, the work had been proceeding. And to anyone who has been engaged in this kind of task the punctuality with which the parts appeared is a matter of no small wonder. Part I was published on 1 July 1896 and the final part in February 1905. Wright had no intention of allowing the work to drag on indefinitely. He had set himself a limit of ten years. During those ten years he achieved the regular publication of the parts as promised, and indeed in 1902 was so well ahead of the work that he was able to increase output to four parts a year. This, of course, could not have been done without much hard work and a kind of ruthless pressing onwards all the time. The rules for the workshop were strict. The hours were from 9 a.m. to 1 p.m. and from 2.30 p.m. to 5.30 p.m. on four afternoons a week. Work in the mornings was continuous. In the afternoons there was a break of fifteen minutes for tea, an idea which Wright yielded to with some reluctance at first but an institution which he soon came to enjoy. So much so that he insisted on supplying the cake himself (with strawberries in June) and often allowed the conversation to be prolonged well beyond the statutory limit.

Thus the *English Dialect Dictionary* got finished. It had cost approximately £25000 to publish, and had occupied ten years of Wright's life. Its six volumes, the last including a supplement and an English dialect grammar, are printed pretty well on the lines of the better-known *Oxford Dictionary*. Each headword is followed by an indication of the pronunciation along exact modern lines. Then follows a list of the localities where the word occurs. Here English and Scottish counties are usually specified, and indeed sometimes also Irish counties, though here and there vaguer terms like 'Ulster' are all we have to go on. Then there is a list (sometimes very long) of varying forms for different localities. Next there follows the meaning or meanings, and finally actual examples from texts or oral notation, without which, of course, no adequate dictionary is complete. The sources for the *Dictionary* are set out separately in a classified list, county by county, with sections for 'colonial', 'American', etc., while for Ireland about 100 works of one kind or another are listed.

The main effect of looking through the *English Dialect Dictionary* is a sobering one. To illustrate this I propose to tell you about a small experiment I carried out. Joyce's *English as we Speak it in Ireland* concludes with a long list entitled 'Vocabulary and Index', which we must presume consists of words and phrases he considered typically Anglo-Irish. From this list I picked out about fifty items. My criterion was words I would use quite casually or habitually myself in ordinary conversation, together with some I would not consider part of my ordinary vocabulary but which I might use on special occasions in particular contexts. Here are a few: *collogue, contrairy, leather* (in the sense of 'beat', which Joyce derives from Irish *leadraim*), *lief, mitch, plawmaws, poteen, ruction, scran (bad scran to you), signs on it, stim, yoke* (in the sense of any kind of apparatus). Of these *plawmaws* and *poteen,* coming as they do from Gaelic words, are given by Wright as limited to Ireland, though no doubt understood elsewhere. The rest, with the possible exception of *yoke* in the sense specified, are quite general in English dialects in England.

This is a small and random sample, and indeed further search would reveal additional English words used in special senses in Ireland. For instance *bring* replacing *take* is given for Ireland only, *close* is not given in the sense of 'sultry (day)', *cog,* though given in the meaning 'cheat, deceive' does not appear in the sense of 'copy', which it had exclusively in my Dublin schooldays, and *cracked* is not given in the sense of 'mad', though *crack-brained* is. Yet cases like these are far outnumbered by those where a typically Irish word or usage is also found in one or more English dialects. This all boils down to saying that in Anglo-Irish we simply have a non-standard form of English which shares a large number of its special features with English dialects elsewhere.

The study of Anglo-Irish is still proceeding, and this essay would be incomplete without some mention of the work that has been done in recent years. I shall deal only with two scholars. They have both made contributions to this book.

Mr. G. B. Adams, of the Ulster Folk Museum, has shown us how complex the linguistic situation is in the north, with its mixture of Elizabethan English and Scots English. Mr. Adams has contributed a number of articles on the subject to the learned periodicals. In 1964 he edited the important work *Ulster Dialects, an introductory symposium,* containing articles on the two main forms of Anglo-Irish in Ulster, on the distribution of dialectal features generally, and an important bibliography. With this work we have come a long way from Joyce's 'essentially a subject for popular treatment'. The publications of our northern colleagues are for the serious scholar, and with them, together with two works I have yet to mention, Anglo-Irish studies may be said to have fallen into step with modern linguistics.

For the rest of Ireland we have the work of Professor P. L. Henry. Indeed, he has not neglected the north either, being a contributor to the *Ulster Dialects* I have already mentioned. As evidenced by his *Anglo-Irish Dialect of North Roscommon,* published in 1957, Professor Henry likes to operate close to the Gaelic fringe, in districts where speakers are removed from their Irish-speaking ancestors by only a few generations. So that the Irish influence shows through all the time, particularly in the matter of pronunciation, but also quite notably in grammar, syntax and idiom. A further contribution of Professor Henry's is his *Linguistic Survey of Ireland, preliminary report,* published in 1958. This is in fact a good deal more than a mere report, for it deals in some detail with all aspects of Anglo-Irish, geographical distribution, history, phonetics, grammar and syntax. As Professor Henry himself says, the object is to 'exhibit the structure and main facts of current Anglo-Irish in its various local forms, to identify the various dialects, and to delimit these — this by a comparative study of grammatical and lexical features'. I have already mentioned that Professor Henry, in his Roscommon book, is concerned with the English of an area not far removed from the Gaelic hinterland. This comes out strongly too in his *Report,* where he suggests that the English of these parts may enable us to get some idea of the Irish originally spoken there. For the sound-system of Roscommon English, as described in Professor Henry's book, is in all its essentials an Irish Gaelic one, and this applies very largely also in the case of grammar and idiom.

Where one language is replaced by another there must at some stage be bilingualism, and this inevitably means that there is never total loss of the speech-habits of the earlier language or total adoption of those of the later. A few years ago Professor Wagner published his *Linguistic Atlas* for those parts of Ireland where Irish is still spoken. By examining the English of the districts adjoining these areas, Professor Henry claims, it may be possible to confirm and extend Professor Wagner's findings. It is an interesting prospect.

DIALECT AND LOCAL ACCENT

GERALD P. DELAHUNTY

Until recently linguists and non-linguists alike would have defined 'dialect' in much the same words as the Oxford English Dictionary does, as 'one of the subordinate forms or varieties of a language arising from local peculiarities of vocabulary, pronunciation and idiom'. In general, linguists would have objected only to the qualification 'subordinate' in this definition by claiming that to them one set of language forms is quite as important as another. Similarly, in its definition by the O.E.D., accent is stated to 'consist mainly in a prevailing quality of tone, or in a peculiar alteration of pitch, but may include mispronunciation of vowels or consonants, misplacing of stress and misinflection of a sentence. The locality of a speaker is generally clearly marked by this kind of accent'. The linguists would have protested most strongly at the pejorative prefix in 'mispronunciation', 'misplacing of stress' and 'misinflection'. They would have discounted any favouritism amongst accents and proclaimed equality of treatment for all.

Such simple and pious sentiments, however, belie two methodological biases inherent in their approaches to dialects and accents. The first of these arises from the linguist's basic acceptance of at least part of the non-technical meaning of the terms, that is, certain forms or groups of forms were regarded as a norm and others as deviations from it. This led to the collecting of items of phonology or lexicon from dialects which differed from the standard dialect merely because they differed. This collection was based rather more on an interest, dating from the beginning of the last century, in traditional folkways, and not in any theoretical concern about the nature of human language and its organisation of diversity. The second bias stemmed from a deep concern with the development of a powerful theory of language which systematically ignored, with extraordinarily productive results, differences observable between speakers of the same language. These differences were placed by many theoreticians outside their immediate, or indeed, proper, view of language, as unimportant variations unrelated to a person's capacity to speak his native language.

Both of these points of view are coming together, in modified forms, in ways which many linguists hope will give a new impetus to a wider and deeper concern about language. The hybrid discipline which undertakes to investigate these matters has generally been called Sociolinguistics or less frequently, the Sociology of Language.

In order to see why this is so let us look again at the dictionary definitions of dialect and accent. The most important thing to be noticed about each is that they bring together linguistic features with social features or meanings. 'Dialect is a manner of speech peculiar to or characteristic of a particular person or class' and the 'locality of a speaker is generally clearly marked by his accent'. And while dialect refers to 'peculiarities of vocabulary, pronunciation and idiom' accent refers only to pronunciation. Both, therefore, reflect two complementary features, locality and social class, so that sociologically and linguistically the concept 'accent' is entailed by the concept 'dialect', and in general, linguists have worked with the latter for all of their investigations.

It is important to notice from these two definitions that dialects and accents are regarded as deviant in some way. There would seem to be a form of speech which is not a dialect, so that certain people would seem to be able to speak without an accent. And from the point of view of the non-linguist this is, of course, true. Generally, those who speak the standard variety of a language are regarded as having no accent, but if one is a Corkman or a Londoner it is not remarkable either if one has a Cork or London accent while at home. However, it is precisely this quality of being remarkable which distinguishes the non-linguist's conception of dialect and accent from the linguist's conception of these. For the linguist, all varieties of a language are remarkable, or problematical, and therefore even those people who are thought to speak without an accent are really a contradiction in terms. It is one of the jobs of the investigating sociolinguist to discover just who these people are, and what they have in common with each other, in exactly the same way as he must discover what other dialect speakers have in common.

In the second half of the last century the study of dialect differences became a major part of linguistic inquiry. Using techniques borrowed from the geographers the dialectologists traced the limits of the occurrences of many lexical and phonological items in many of the languages of Europe and published their findings in a series of dialect atlases. Those areas in which the occurrence of a phenomenon was reported were enclosed in boundary lines called isoglosses, marked on the maps in the same way as isotherms enclose areas which have the same mean temperature. It was frequently found that isogloss lines clustered about an area which was recognisable as an historical unit in its own right. In Germany, for example, many isogloss lines clustered about the borders of the old electoral states. However, it was frequently found that the isoglosses divided such states into two or more sectors. The dialectologists who mapped these items in terms of their geographical distribution explained discontinuities in terms of ancient migrations, or barriers to communication, or as free variants. Variation, therefore, was to be accounted for as a function of distance: that is, geographical or social distance from each other led people to use different words for the same thing, different sounds in the same words and so on. It was observed that while the dialects of a language have much in common with each other they are not individually homogeneous units.

Similarly, within the speech of a single speaker variation will be observable, and can be a function of the interaction in which the speaker is participating. The variation will be correlatable with the relative socioeconomic statuses of the participants, the place in which the interaction is occurring, its purpose, and many other factors. Thus in everyday life people change their accents and dialects, that is, they may alternate between language varieties for many reasons. They may switch between their vernacular dialect or accent and an accent more or less prestigious than that. Similarly, in the course of their lives, people may substitute one dialect for another as they move from place to place, or from class to class. The number, or range, of such varieties that a person can utilise has been called the speaker's 'linguistic repertoire', and the extent of this repertoire may have considerable significance for a person's educability and general societal mobility.

These kinds of observations gave rise to a number of theatres of attack, which represent the various points of view within sociolinguistics, all focusing on different facets of the same problem. Some emphasise the linguistic aspect and others the sociological aspects, but each tries to account for variation within language and for speakers' selections from amongst the available sets of forms. Those who have tackled the linguistic part have faced the problem of inventing a grammar (essentially a model conforming to mathematical rules) which can adequately describe and account for language variation at all levels. And those who emphasise the sociological component investigate the societal factors influencing the speaker's choice and range of variants. From this point of view it can be seen that the dialectologists of the last century, and until recently, represent an initiating step toward a more fully developed theory, or set of theories, which will explain the complex interaction between language and social living. It would be useful, therefore, to try to uncover those factors which investigators, interested in developing these theories and the methodologies to go with them, have discussed in the literature.

The first point to be made is that accent and dialect are not precise and defined units of language. In this regard they are similar to the term 'a language' itself. In linguistic, rather than sociological terms it is often impossible to draw the boundaries between one accent and another, between one dialect and another, or even between two languages. If only linguistic criteria, such as phonetics or syntax or lexicon, are taken into account, then it may prove impossible to precisely differentiate between pairs of accents or dialects. If the problem is stated in a different way it might seem more clear. Considering that accents and dialects are types of units within a language or between languages, we must, therefore, assume that these dialects and accents share a great many features; but on how many features must two varieties differ before they become distinct accents or dialects? If, for example, the only difference between two persons' speech in Dublin was that one of them habitually said 'I seen' where the other habitually said 'I saw', would these two people have to be judged to be speakers of different dialects? If they do not, then how many differences would have to be observable between them before they would in fact be judged to be speaking separate dialects? From the point of view of the methods used by the older dialectologists to catalogue these differences, this is the only type of question which can be asked about the relationships between dialects.

A number of areas of inquiry do arise from this question. Firstly, it is obvious that dialects are contrastive units in the same way as languages are, and therefore the identifying features are ascribed salience in a socially functional way. Thus the differences between some dialects may be considerably smaller, linguistically, than between one of them and another, or even in comparison with variation within a single dialect. Certain variant items, therefore, are more typical or are assumed to be more characteristic, of certain dialects than of others. For example, one of the features most often cited as typical of Dublin English is that of vowel breaking to give a disyllabic structure in words such as 'room' [rɨuem] and in many other words where a similar breaking of a close or half-close vowel before a voiced consonant occurs. There are other features, such as devoicing of word-final voiced consonants in polysyllabic words, which are not noticed by people generally and certainly not cited as typical of any types of Dublin speech, or of Dublin speech as a whole, even though they may be, as the devoicing feature is, far more widespread in the city than the vowel breaking is.

The most usual types of features cited as markers of a person's place of origin are phonological. Thus a person has a Dublin or a Cork or a Belfast accent if certain sounds occur in his speech which are perceived to be characteristic of whichever place is in question. In Ireland there are only a small number of distinct accents that are generally and consistently recognised by the adult population, even though many people will be able to make much finer judgements, such as people who can discriminate between five or even six distinct Dublin varieties. These major countrywide accents seem to be those of Dublin, Cork, Northern Ireland and Donegal, of Kerry, perhaps, and of the Midlands, and finally the one which is referred to as not being an accent at all. This latter is used by people from widely-separated parts of the country who share many features of education, life-style and assumptions. This could be referred to as the standard Irish pronunciation of English or Hiberno-English.

The second area of inquiry is concerned with the effects of being classified as a speaker of a particular dialect on peoples' judgements of the speaker's personality, background and capabilities, and the truth of these judgements. These will be discussed below.

I have not yet attempted an alternate definition of the terms 'dialect' and 'accent' to the dictionary accounts quoted in the opening, and this is because many workers in the field have used the terms, or at least the term 'dialect' in inconsistent and often contradictory ways. However, it will now be obvious to the reader that certain concerns must be fitted into any proposed definition. I have so far indicated briefly what is involved in the non-technical use of the terms and outlined some approaches to a more penetrating study of variation. I would like now to turn to some other points of view which have been touched upon already. The starting point for these approaches is that the primary area of attention is not the dialect or accent but rather the speech community to which it is ascribed. The problems of deciding upon the boundaries of the target community has been the subject of an impressive volume of work — particularly that of the Norwegian anthropologist Frederik Barth. The solution to this problem might also help solve the linguists' problem of when to stop checking on variant forms. The solution seems to lie in the concept of reciprocally ascribed group membership. By this I mean that if I agree with other Irishmen and non-Irishmen that I am an Irishman, I have had ascribed to me and I ascribe to myself membership of a particular group. This ascription also applies within a group, where a person is deemed to belong to a particular subgroup and in turn believes himself to belong to that. This solution would be fine if there were not people who belong to more than one group at a time, or to groups which form in areas of contact between languages. The subject of this paper is essentially concerned with the marking of groups of many sizes by linguistic means. Certain features in the speech of members of a group come to be regarded as being used typically by just those group members and thus any speakers displaying them will be regarded as members of that group, and whatever the hearer feels, or has been taught to think about the members of a particular group he will associate with the marking linguistic features and any people who use them. A very considerable amount of research has been carried out on this topic in Canada, in Israel and in England, to name but a few locations. The results have been very consistent and fascinating. Very briefly I will outline the results of the English experiments.

A group of subjects in different age brackets are asked to listen to a piece of prose read in Standard English with Received Pronunciation and in a variety of regional and foreign accents. The subjects are then asked to evaluate in turn, the different speakers on certain personality characteristics such as intelligence, generosity, sense of humour, ambition, self-confidence, industriousness, social status and some others of similar type. The judgements turn out to be quite consistent and perhaps somewhat predictable. The Standard English speaker was rated as more intelligent, more self-confident and of higher status than the speakers of the regional varieties, who were felt to be more generous, more good-humoured but of lower social status. The features thus seem to fall into two natural divisions, with the speakers of the regional varieties being evaluated more highly on features of sociableness, while the speakers of Standard English are more highly evaluated on achievement features. Very similar results were obtained in Canada where Canadian French and English were used as stimuli. These results do not at all indicate that French Canadians or speakers of regional varieties of English are not capable of high achievement in terms of status or intellectual attainment, or that Received Pronunciation speakers or speakers of Canadian English are less sociable than other speakers. But it does mean that the subjects that rated them feel that these are ascribed in this ratio as a result of general societal values attached to the different types of speech because these are presumed to be true of those groups who maintain these separate speech varieties and are recognisable by them. From the point of view of this methodology two things are held constant: firstly, the different varieties to be evaluated are all spoken by a single person and secondly, the content of what is said in the speech samples can have no effect because the speaker reads the same passage of neutral prose for each sample. But the more regionally marked speech is, then the less favourably it will be judged in terms of core societal values, especially on those values upon which societal prestige is based. Another interesting finding in this regard has been that raters are willing to extrapolate from these stimuli which differ only on phonetic features, to judgements of the syntactic or morphological characteristics of the samples. In other words, the more distant a sample sounds from standard the more likely it is to be judged to contain syntactic and morphological items that are used only in the non-standard varieties even though these were categorically excluded from it.

The second area of inquiry referred to above concerns the question of what, if any, real substance there is to the evaluations made of the speakers.

Since the early sixties Professor Basil Bernstein, in a series of studies of class differences in England, has investigated speakers' abilities to express different types of ideas and experiences. He claims to have established a firm correlation between certain types of language variety and the ability of speakers to express certain types of ideas and to communicate particular kinds of experience. Bernstein isolated a continuum of linguistic organisation, the polarities of which he calls Restricted and Elaborated codes. These codes must not be identified with either accent or dialect, for reasons which will become clear in a few moments. Bernstein has associated this linguistic continuum with other social continua and a very definite pattern has emerged. The code types are related to types of social organisation within social groups, for example, with types of social control, with types of family organisation, with role systems and with communication systems. The Restricted pole is highly correlated with groups where social control is dependent upon authority derived from a person's position within the group. This applies mainly to family types but is applicable also to any closed communication system where the decisions are not usually open to discussion. A restricted code, therefore, does not allow for a great deal of individual expression or dissension from imposed decisions. Elaborated codes are associated with more open types of control which allow for considerable discussion within the decision-making process, and speakers who control an elaborated code are in a position to express their individual opinions and thoughts rather more than those speakers limited to a restricted code. Bernstein claims to have proved that certain social classes, especially the lower socioeconomic groups in England, very often control only restricted codes and that as a result their ability to benefit from a formal school situation is severely limited. This seems to be because certain types of logical relationships are unlikely to be coded. The value of restricted codes is hypothesised to lie in the assumption that they have evolved rather more for the expression of group solidarity than for the expression of a person's individual point of view. On the other hand elaborated codes have evolved for the expression of individuated experiences and for the verbal exploration of unique approaches and interpretations, and are, therefore, assumed to be much more suited to the school situation. Because of the lack of definiteness surrounding the term dialect it might be assumed that standard dialects and elaborated codes are one and the same thing. But the concept of code does not allow for this identification. In precisely the same way, the non-technical term dialect does not correspond to restricted code either, nor are dialect speakers necessarily limited to this type of expression. What is likely to occur is that for dialect speakers who control both restricted and elaborated codes, their elaborated code will probably be identified linguistically as conforming to the rules of the standard language. This, however, is not a necessary or inevitable distribution of resources, but it is very likely to be true of the English-speaking culture areas and perhaps of western European culture generally. From this it will be obvious that, potentially, a dialect can include both types of code and that neither need be identical, linguistically or sociolinguistically, with the standard dialect of the language to which they belong.

Many researchers, however, are critical of Bernstein's interpretation of his data, and for many good reasons. It has been found that the factors involved in reduced educability lie rather in the linguistic, and especially in the sociolinguistic differences between the middle and lower classes. American researchers have found that black children from lower socioeconomic groups who have been judged by psychologists and teachers to be below average intelligence and in need of remedial speech lessons, often turn out to be skilful and creative speakers when observed in interaction with their peers. The range of varieties over which an individual has control will be an accurate indicator of the social groups and functions in which he can and probably does participate. What seems to be happening, therefore, is that the children from the lower classes, or from any class or group not instrumental in the organisation of the educational environments, and therefore in no position to form their sociolinguistic rules, will be able to utilise the system only to the extent that they control the variety appropriate to it.

But so long as no effort is made to understand and accommodate the sociolinguistic system which the children bring to the schools they will be unable, in frighteningly many cases, to attain command of the necessary language variety and will be denied rightful access to full educational opportunity. It is obvious, therefore, that in reality it is the alien testing or educational situation to which the children cannot respond, and not any inherent defect either of themselves or of their language which allows such judgements to be made of them. Bernstein's work has been carried out in just such a controlled setting, and in all probability it is this which is responsible for the reduced range of verbal expression he has been able to elicit. Grave doubts therefore arise with regard to the validity of much of his thesis.

Considerably more research is needed before any final decision can be made regarding the relative capacities of languages and language varieties to code comparable meanings. The recent revival of interest in Pidgin and Creole languages provides much support for the point of view that what can be coded in one language can be coded in another, more or less economically.

From this it can be seen that if we simply catalogue

the forms of the dialects without reference to the functions to which they are put, and the relationships between them in the speech community, we are discovering nothing of value. It is like classifying dogs according to the names given them by their owners and expecting to break the genetic code. By this line of reasoning we are forced once again to the concept of the speech community as the basic unit of sociolinguistic investigation.

Hymes has defined the speech community as one which 'shares rules for the conduct and interpretation of speech and rules for the interpretation of at least one linguistic variety. Both conditions are necessary.' The term variety here refers to a form of speech whose use is restricted to selection for a particular function such as negotiating, courting, academic discussion, and at least in modern society, very many other types of function.

We are now in a position to make some tentative divisions of speech forms in a community. As in all matters linguistic it is contrastive units that are significant to us. Thus one language contrasts with another, or within a single language area, dialects contrast with each other. And it is only by the ascription of this status of contrast with each other that linguistic differences in fact become accents or dialects. A dialect from this point of view is potentially a separate language and the term is used in historical linguistics to refer to the separate descendant languages of a reconstructed or even (in some form) extant parent language. Thus Latin and Greek and Sanskrit are all in this sense dialects of the Indo-European language from which they have evolved. There is, besides, a further reason for looking upon dialects as potential languages and this has to do with the fullness to which dialects present speakers with total alternative sociolinguistic systems. A dialect area may in fact present an alternative social structure more or less completely to the embedding community. Certain dialects may organise the rules of interpretation or codes in different ways, or as I said before, some dialects may possess certain codes but have to borrow others from alternative sources. Differences in code are not dependent essentially on differences in phonetics or on the selection of different words or morphemes, but mainly upon the rules for interpreting what is said in any given context. For example, what can be said on very formal occasions is quite limited in content, and therefore predictable, and must be said in 'very correct' speech, or, let us say, in standard English. This would be a case of restricted code and it would be a mistake to interpret what is said under such circumstances in the same way as one might interpret the same passage of speech in, for example, a conversation between two close friends. These are coding differences, and dialects differ in terms of the coding resources they possess, without any sharing or codes. The usual configuration is that dialects will establish their own restricted codes, or in Labov's term (not exactly synonymous), vernacular, which may very well be uninterpretable to people not native or adopted members of the group. At another level there exists a further set of contrasting speech forms which I have mentioned before. These are called varieties or registers and are selected as appropriate for use in specific types of situations. Dialects may differ in the number of varieties they entail and may also differ in the forms they use to mark these varieties. The relationship between registers and codes is somewhat problematical and there would seem to be some redundancy in the concepts if they are taken together. In general it is likely that registers are a set within the elaborated codes of a language or dialect.

It will be obvious to the reader that we are dealing with language phenomena at a level of organisation with each other far in advance of that of the sentence level, and with meanings conveyed, not by direct reference, but by the accumulation of features. The meanings themselves will differ in details from language to language and from dialect to dialect, but it does seem, at least in those countries where a standard dialect has developed, that the evaluation of speech types is closely associated with the social conditions of those who speak these types, or at least with the beliefs about those circumstances and their position within the value system of the total community. Why is it then that highly stigmatised speech forms persist and are used, even by people who know and can use the more prestigious forms? The answer to this seems to be in the positive evaluation placed on these forms by the subcommunity that uses them and, as in the cases outlined before, even by the larger community. As I mentioned earlier, this positive evaluation seems most often to be associated with social cohesion rather than personal achievement, and is connected with the dialect speaking group's desire to maintain their separate identity as a group. They therefore use their distinctive speech forms as an integrating mechanism between members of the group and as a segregating mechanism against outsiders.

Two further concepts are of considerable importance in the discussion of speech types. The first of these has to do with the internal organisation of the phonological, lexical and syntactic features on a code or dialect or variety. Certain items occur only in conjunction with other items; for example, one does not expect to hear a mixture such as: 'I beg to inform your excellency tha' I done ezakly wha' I wuz tol'.' Such a combination breaks the cooccurrence restrictions of the language at various levels. So it can be seen that it is in contrasting sets of features, with quite precise rules of cooccurrence, that languages mark off significant coding or varietal distinctions, and it is by the alternation of one such set for another as circumstances demand that contrasting social meanings are conveyed.

It has recently become possible to add a precise linguistic dimension to the essentially sociological judgement that two varieties, dialects or languages are in fact different entities. In some very fascinating work carried out in Norway, John Gumperz and Jan-Petter Blom were able to show that linguistic differences between dialects conform to observable and describable restrictions. These observations by Gumperz and Blom are based on a concept developed by Labov in a major study of the English of New York city. In that study Labov proposed the concept of the 'variable', a sociolinguistic unit of phonology which recognises that the articulation of phonemes varies within a certain range as a function of changing social circumstances and speakers, and interactional goals and assumptions. Within any speech community the allowable ranges, and the marking social factors will display a striking consistency, both in the selection of the phonetic values of the variables and in the societal judgements accorded them. Gumperz and Blom, working on the relative positions of one of Norway's standard languages and the dialect of an area called Rana, found that these, Bokmål and Ranamål respectively, are describable in terms of a single grammatical system, but are differentiated by variable type components which entail phonology, lexicon and morphology. Recent studies such as these have had a profound effect on the understanding of linguistic change and the mechanisms whereby items move upwards or downwards in terms of the prestige accorded them by the speech community in the process of selection of the different values of the variables.

In a study in 1971 Bailey hypothesised that variation in language is characterisable by a rule which sometimes operates and sometimes does not, and that the linguistic environments of the item involved can be implicationally scaled against the set of groups using the item in such a way that those environments in which the rule is variable imply, on the one hand, environments in which the rule is categorically present, and on the other hand, environments in which it is categorically absent. These scales are constructed by listing the sets of linguistic environments along one axis of a matrix and a set of either geographical or social features along the other, and then the types of occurrence of the rule, that is, categorical or variable presence or categorical absence, are plotted within the matrix and the contents can be shown to form an implicational scale, so that a language change operates by successive categoricalisations of the environments in which the rule operates. The implicational nature of these scales offers some insight into the way human beings organise language variation, that is as implicational sets.

Labov has proposed an alternative model to account for this variation. He considers each rule to be associated with a probability coefficient which will predict how frequently the rule will be applied (or not applied). The environments in which the rule can possibly apply are differentially weighted to indicate the relative degree to which each environment favours or inhibits application of the rule. David Sankoff has proved that there is no mathematical reason to prefer Bailey's hypothesis to Labov's, as long as an inevitable degree of scaling error is accepted in the implicational model.

The incorporation of either of these two models of variation into the Chomskyian theory of linguistic competence would constitute a major revision of the current thinking on language and would have vital ramifications for psycholinguistics, especially in the study of children's acquisition of their first language. Indeed there is some indication that such a revision is slowly taking place.

Again it is shown to be imperative to recognise the necessity, not just of observing the contrast between pairs of items, but rather between sets of items showing a high degree of internal organisation. Randomness in language is quite meaningless and free variation is uninteresting, if it occurs, and the weight of the evidence seems to throw considerable doubt upon that possibility. The proper study of language is the study of system and not the study of the distribution of single items for their own sake.

The perspective on language that I have been discussing has many important ramifications for the study of bilingualism and the language changes that occur in multilingual situations. It has always been known that contiguous or superposed languages borrow from each other on many levels, and by regarding languages which have been in contact with each other for a considerable period of time as relatable to multi-dialectal situations, it becomes possible to understand the social organisation of language choice and the distribution of codes and registers, as well as the implications of this organisation for the forms maintained by the speakers and the relationships between them. Gumperz has satisfactorily shown that where languages have been in contact for a long time, and where the groups in the bilingual community must communicate frequently with each other, then in exactly the same way as two dialects of a single language share a great deal of their structure and are related to each other in organised ways, so also do two languages converge and evolve toward ever greater degrees of sharing of rules and structure, until, as in Gumperz' site in India, the only difference between the languages is that they possess two sets of words, and all other features are shared. Thus when a person is speaking one language he selects from one set of words, and when he is speaking the other language then he chooses from the other set, but the rules of sentence construction, the semantics, the phonological rules and the phonetic rules are all shared, even though from the point of view of a comparative grammarian the two languages, as in India, may belong to two language families. Obviously Gumperz found exactly what he was looking for. He chose his site very carefully, taking into account the social, historical and linguistic set-up there, and as a result he discovered an advanced stage of convergence in stable multilingualism. It was, however, by looking at the reorganisation of the constituent subsystems of the languages that his insights derive. He has proved that languages can be almost totally identical and yet, for the members of the speech community, satisfy their need to mark off and maintain differences between subgroups.

From the point of view of the language situation in Ireland, this type of more theoretically oriented language study should add a necessary dimension to the discussion of language purity and national distinctiveness. It should also lead to the proper funding of valuable linguistic research which would supercede the anecdotal coverage that language has been getting since the end of the last century.

Many foreigners, especially German scholars, have come to Ireland and done much valuable work on both Irish and English in recent years, and they have used highly-developed methodologies. We might profitably begin to think about what it is that they find so interesting here. We ought to be concerned with a number of points of view. Firstly, and most importantly, we ought to be concerned with the development and testing of new and interesting hypotheses concerning language and social life, and secondly, with the proper exploration of our own bilingual situation and its typological uniqueness. It is only with a strict regard for the purely scientific value of such exploration that any application in the life and activities of the society becomes possible and progressive rather than inhibiting and destructive, as they have been in the past. It is one of the paradoxes of science that actual problems get truly solved only in the context of ongoing free inquiry, and it is only by making problematical what has seemed to be factual and accepted that any understanding becomes possible.

BIBLIOGRAPHY

Alatis, James E. (ed.):
   (1969) *Report of the 20th Annual Round Table Meeting on Linguistics and Language Studies* (Georgetown University Press).

Bailey, C. J.-N.
   (1973) 'The Patterning of Language Variation', in Bailey and Robinson (1973).

Bailey, Richard W. and Robinson, Jay L. (eds.)
   (1973) *Varieties of Present-day English* (New York, Macmillan).

Barth, Frederik
   (1972) 'Ethnic Processes on the Pathan-Baluch Boundary', in Gumperz and Hymes (1972).

Bernstein, Basil
   (1961) 'Aspects of Language and Learning in the Genesis of the Social Process', in Hymes (1964).
   (1962) *Class Codes and Control,* Vol. 1 (London, Routledge and Kegan Paul).
   (1972) 'A Sociolinguistic Approach to Socialisation: With Some Reference to Educability', in Gumperz and Hymes (1972).

Bloomfield, Leonard
   (1933) *Language* (New York).

Blom, Jan-Petter, and Gumperz, John J.
   (1972) 'Social Meaning in Linguistic Structures: Code Switching in Norway', in Gumperz and Hymes (1972).

Bright, William O.
   (1960) 'Social Dialect and Language History', in Hymes (1964).

Bull, William A.
(1955) 'The Use of Vernacular Languages in Fundamental Education', in *International Journal of American Linguistics*, 21. Reprinted in Hymes (1964).

Cicourel, Aaron V.
(1972) 'Cross-Modal Communication', in Shuy (1972).

Conklin, Harold C.
(1959) 'Linguistic Play in its Cultural Context', in *Language*, 35. Reprinted in Hymes (1964).

Ervin-Tripp, Susan
(1972) 'On Sociolinguistic Rules: Alternation and Cooccurrence', in Gumperz and Hymes (1972).

Ferguson, Charles A.
(1959) 'Diglossia', in *Word*, 15. Reprinted in Hymes (1964).

Fischer, John L.
(1958) 'Social Influences in the Choice of a Linguistic Variant', in *Word*, 14. Reprinted in Hymes (1964).

Frenden, Robert, and Lambert, Wallace E.
(1972) 'Speech Style and Scholastic Success: The Tentative Relationships and Possible Implications for Lower Social Class Children', in Shuy (1972).

Garvin, Paul L.
(1959) 'The Standard Language Problem; Concepts and Methods', in *Anthropological Linguistics*, 1 (2).

Gumperz, John J.
(1961) 'Speech Variation and the Study of Indian Civilisation', in *American Anthropologist*, 63. Reprinted in Hymes (1964).
(1969) 'Communication in Multilingual Societies', in Tyler (1969).
—— and Herasimchuk, Eleanor
(1972) 'The Conversational Analysis of Social Meaning: A Study of Classroom Interaction', in Shuy (1972).
—— and Hymes, Dell. (eds.)
(1972) *Directions in Sociolinguistics: The Ethnography of Communication* (Holt, Rinehart and Winston, Inc.).

Hymes, Dell.

(1972) 'Models of the Interaction of Language and Social Life', in Gumperz and Hymes (1972).

(1964) (ed.) *Language in Culture and Society: A Reader in Linguistics and Anthropology* (Harper and Row).

(1971) (ed.) *Pidginisation and Creolisation of Languages* (Cambridge University Press).

John, Vera P.

(1972) 'Sociolinguistic Perspectives and Education', in Shuy (1972).

Kreidler (ed.)

(1965) *Report of the 18th Annual Meeting on Linguistics and Language Studies* (Georgetown University Press).

Labov, William

(1965) 'On the Mechanism of Linguistic Change', in Kreidler (1965). Reprinted in part in Gumperz and Hymes (1972).

(1966) *The Social Stratification of English in New York City* (Washington D.C. Centre for Applied Linguistics).

(1969a) 'The Logic of Non-Standard English', in Alatis (1969).

(1969b) 'Contraction, Deletion and Inherent Variability of the English Copula', in *Language, 45*.

(1971) 'The Notion of "System" in Creole Studies', in Hymes (1971).

(1972) *Language in the Inner City* (Philadelphia, University of Pennsylvania Press).

(1973) *Sociolinguistic Patterns* (Philadelphia, University of Pennsylvania Press).

McDavid, Raven I., Jr.

(1948) 'Post vocalic /r/ in South Carolina: A Social Analysis', in *American Speech, 23*. Reprinted in Hymes (1964).

Sankoff, David, and Rousseau, Pascale

(1973) 'A Method for Assessing Variable Rule and Implicational Analysis of Linguistic Variation', International Conference on Computers in the Humanities (University of Minnesota, Minneapolis, 1973).

Shuy, Roger W.
(1972) *Report of the 23rd Annual Round Table Meeting on Linguistics and Language Studies* (Georgetown University Press).

Trager, George L.
(1939) ' "Cottonwood" = "Tree": A Southwestern Linguistic Trait', in *International Journal of American Linguistics*. Reprinted in Hymes (1964).

Tyler, Stephen A.
(1969) *Cognitive Anthropology* (Holt, Rinehart and Winston, Inc.).

THE PLEASURES OF GAELIC LITERATURE
Edited by John Jordan.

What is the purpose of this book? Obviously it is not
addressed primarily to those who are habitual readers of
Irish, though one might hope that familiar texts might be
approached freshly in the light of personal insights from
commentators, all of them involved in the creation or
appreciation of literature. When we set about making
this Thomas Davis Lecture series, we had in mind an
audience whose attitudes to Irish are neither hostile nor
committedly enthusiastic, an audience part of which never
arrived at an approach towards Gaelic literature other
than in the most primitive critical terms, and part of which
might never think of reading a book in Irish with the same
high seriousness as they would bring to a book in English
or any other European language.

It may be hard for many dedicated teachers to recognise the situation whereby even pupils fluent in Irish
may have an almost apologetic attitude towards literature
in Irish. We hope that this book may help to defrost this
kind of literary indifferentism.

John Jordan

The Contributors:
John Jordan
Máire Cruise O'Brien
Pearse Hutchinson
Séamus Deane
Eoghan O Tuairisc
Breandán O hEithir
Brendan Kennelly
Tomás de Bhaldraithe
Seán O Faoiláin